The Story of Spanis

Charles H. Caffin

Alpha Editions

This edition published in 2024

ISBN : 9789362997142

Design and Setting By
Alpha Editions
www.alphaedis.com
Email - info@alphaedis.com

As per information held with us this book is in Public Domain.
This book is a reproduction of an important historical work. Alpha Editions uses the best technology to reproduce historical work in the same manner it was first published to preserve its original nature. Any marks or number seen are left intentionally to preserve its true form.

Contents

CHAPTER I THE STORY OF THE NATION ....- 1 -

CHAPTER II CHARACTERISTICS OF SPANISH PAINTING ....- 14 -

CHAPTER III A PANORAMIC VIEW Part I: To the End of the Sixteenth Century ....- 24 -

CHAPTER IV A PANORAMIC VIEW Part II: Seventeenth Century to the Present Day. ....- 33 -

CHAPTER V DOMENCO THEOTOCOPULI (EL GRECO) ....- 41 -

CHAPTER VI VELASQUEZ ....- 60 -

CHAPTER VII MAZO ....- 81 -

CHAPTER VIII CARREÑO ....- 88 -

CHAPTER IX RIBERA (LO SPAGNOLETTO) ....- 92 -

CHAPTER X MURILLO ....- 99 -

CHAPTER XI CANO AND ZURBARÁN ....- 108 -

CHAPTER XII GOYA .... - 115 -

A POSTSCRIPT .... - 129 -

CHAPTER I

THE STORY OF THE NATION

IN 1492 the Catholic Sovereigns, Ferdinand and Isabella, entered Granada in triumph. The last stronghold of Moorish dominion, undermined by the dissensions of Islam, fell before the united Christian kingdoms of Léon, Castile and Aragón. Spain became a united country and, in virtue of her protracted struggle of nearly eight hundred years against the infidel, stood forth as the acknowledged and self-conscious Champion of Catholicism. In the same year Columbus, under the patronage of the Catholic Sovereigns discovered the New World. This date, therefore, presents an epoch that completes the past and forms the starting point of a new era. Intimately associated with the subsequent national development and decline is the story of Spanish painting, but it owes most of its peculiar characteristics to the conditions that preceded the country's complete union.

It is always interesting and usually illuminating to picture the historical background out of which the arts of a country have been gradually evolved. But in the case of Spanish painting it is essential. For the art of Spain was, bone and spirit, a part of the Spanish character, shaped and inspired as the latter had been by the racial, historical and geographical conditions out of which it was moulded. Without taking all this into account one cannot understand, much less appreciate sympathetically, the consistently individual character of this school of painting.

. . . .

In the first place one must realise the meaning of the fact that Spain is a mountainous country; not only separated from the rest of Europe, but divided against itself by precipitous barriers. They run in a general way from West to East: abrupt colossal walls of volcanic origin, with a grand sweep of bulk, jagged in sky-line and frequently piled with the chaotic debris of glacial moraines. These are the watersheds of rivers that refuse services to navigation; foaming to flood in the rainy season, shrinking in the drought to sluggish pools amid the rocky bed. They intersect tracts of country that vary from narrow valleys, where cultivation huddles in cherished pockets of soil, to broadly stretching vegas, tablelands and plains, from which by unremitting toil generous harvests may be obtained. Here the vistas are of magnificent extent, circling round one in far reaching sweeps of boldly undulating country, rimmed by nobly designed stretches of smoothly beveled foothills that form advance-posts of the ultimate barrier of the sierras.

It is a little country, only three times the size of England, contracted within itself by natural restrictions, yet planned by nature on a big scale; one that affects the imagination, prompting even more than mountainous countries usually have done to independence, individualism and hardihood. It is a country that seems made for fighting; where a handful of resolute men could maintain themselves tenaciously against enormous odds. In the past they did it in actual warfare; to-day in the pacific fight which this hardy population perpetually keeps up against the extremes of climatic conditions. Though for the most part they still use the agricultural implements that Tubal Cain devised, they have inherited from the Roman and Moorish occupation a system of irrigation and of terracing that puts to shame the happy go lucky methods of farming in many countries which consider themselves superiorly enlightened. The necessary preoccupation with their immediate surroundings and the exclusion from outside influence, early made of this people a nation of individualists, realists and conservatives. So inbred did these qualities become that when the Spaniard mixed with the outer world, as he did particularly in his conquest of the Spanish Main and in his wars with Europe, it was but to become more fixed in his conservatism at home. When he borrowed from abroad, as in his art, it was but to shape and color the acquired impression to his own individualistic and realistic attitude toward life.

. . . .

The earliest inhabitants of the Peninsula are known as Iberians; with whom about 500 B.C., a branch of the Celtic family became amalgamated. These Celtiberians remained in undisputed possession of the country, until they were drawn into the vortex that was stirred by the rivalry of Rome and Carthage. The latter had planted colonies along the south coast, and gradually extended her authority into the interior, dealing as was her wont in a spirit of suspicion and brutality with the natives. The Romans, hot on the trail of their traditional foe, at first suffered decisive reverses. Then it was that Scipio the Younger offered himself to the Senate and People of Rome as general of the war. His father and uncle had been slain in battle in Spain; he desired to avenge their deaths and to crush the enemies of Rome. Though only twenty-four years of age he had the genius of a military leader and of a statesman. While putting heart into the shattered ranks of the Roman veterans and leading them victoriously against the Carthaginians, he adopted towards the Spaniards a policy of confidence and conciliation which won them over to a loyal acceptance of the Roman rule. A similar policy was practised by Suetonius in later years, when Spain had become the battle ground of the rival factions with which Rome was torn. It was continued by Julius Cæsar when he fought out his fight with Pompey on

Spanish soil, and later by Augustus when, having become ruler of the Roman world, he completed pacifically the conquest of Spain.

Henceforth Spain was the most favored, loyal and prosperous province of the Empire. At first the Roman veterans, retiring from military service, married Spanish women and settled down as farmers, introducing gradually the order and scientific method for which the Romans are so justly celebrated. The settled conditions, fertility of the soil, and the beauty of the country in time attracted the wealth and culture of the Capital. Spain became, like "The Province" in the South of France, a field for capitalistic enterprise as well as a resort for those who leaned toward a life of refined leisure. She throve in the arts and sciences and became enriched with some of the finest evidences of the Roman genius for engineering. Her wheatfields fed the proletariat of the Capital and her sons reinforced the ranks of statesmen and men of letters. She became, in the finest sense of the word, more Roman than Italy herself. This period of splendid prosperity lasted for four hundred years, until it was submerged, like the rest of Roman civilization, by the flood of Gothic invasion.

The branch of the German family which overran Spain was that of the Visigoths, who maintained an ascendency and a line of kings for two hundred years. But, although the enervation caused by provincial luxury had rendered the Celtiberian-Roman an easy victim to the vigorous onslaught of the northern race, he was sufficiently tenacious of the original spirit of the mountaineer and of the acquired love of order to avoid the chaos and prostration that overtook the rest of the Empire, and reasserted his instinct for amalgamation. The blend, which ensued and became the Spanish race as it is known to later history, is characteristically represented in the language that was gradually evolved. For this, though overlaid with Northern forms, remains at root Roman. In this hybrid race the Spanish element proved itself to be the most pronounced and enduring. Its conservatism, a phase of the independence and exclusiveness that we have already noted, was conspicuously revealed in the great Arian Controversy which threatened the integrity of the Western Church. The Visigoths alone of all the Germanic family, renounced the "heresy." Reccared, their king, received in consequence the title of the first Catholic Sovereign of Spain. How resolutely subsequent sovereigns clung to this distinction and their subjects conformed to the political and religious obligations that it entailed is one of the most notable features of Spanish history. It seriously affected the national life, its attitude toward other nations and the development and character of Spanish art.

Meanwhile the mingling of blood could not save the Visigothic kingdom from the fate that attended all the Germanic governments which had been established on the ruins of the Empire. It proved no exception to the tendency to disintegrate and thus presented an easy prey to the onslaughts of united Islam.

In less than a hundred years after the death of Mohammed the Moslem faith had spread from Arabia through Syria and Asia Minor to Persia and India, while Westward it had overrun Egypt and penetrated along the northern shore of Africa to the Pillars of Hercules. Hence in 711 A.D. it crossed into Spain. While the leaders, under the generalship of Musa, viceroy of the Omayyad Caliphate of Damascus, were all Arabs, they had enlisted in their army the warlike tribes of Mauritania, the ancient kingdom now represented by Morocco and Algeria. Hence the name of Moors (Mauri) which distinguishes the invaders of Spain. Twenty years sufficed to make them masters of the Peninsula, the little northwestern country of Asturias alone retaining its independence. Twenty years later disintegration crept also into the ranks of the conquerors. Abd-er-Rahman established an independent caliphate in Cordova. His ambition was to raise it to a position in the Western world such as was held by Bagdad, Damascus and Delhi in the East; furthermore to make Cordova the Mecca of the faithful in the West. Thus was begun by this Caliph the Mesquita or chief Mosque, which under succeeding Caliphs was enlarged and beautified until it became a fitting monument of the ideals of Islam in its period of most splendid pride and noblest enlightenment. For nearly three hundred years Cordova was the center of an ordered government, which not only fostered the refinement of the arts and crafts in the cities and spread its network of highly organised agricultural labor throughout the country districts, but also a University of philosophy and science that made it the resort of scholars, not only Moslem but Christian. Cordova, in fact, played a conspicuously brilliant part in that phase of the Moslem ascendency which is apt to be overlooked; its share in perpetuating and advancing the Hellenic culture, which otherwise might have been lost in the Dark Ages succeeding the fall of the Roman Empire.

Meanwhile, the spirit of Christian Spain, though broken, was not crushed. Its stronghold was at first the little kingdom of Asturias. Alfonso I not only resisted conquest but wrested back from the Moor the provinces of Galicia and Cantabria. From the northwest fastnesses of the Peninsula commenced the steady pressure southward, which, while it met with many reverses, was never abandoned until the invader had been driven back to Africa. The story in brief is one of gradual consolidation of the Christian power, accompanied by a corresponding disintegration of the Moslem. Léon becomes united with the other provinces and Castile follows suit; while on the other hand the Caliphate of Cordova becomes broken up into several dynasties. Then, while a rival sect, the Almoravides, arrive from Africa and make war on their co-religionists, Alfonso IV of Castile assumes the title of Emperor and captures Toledo and Valencia. Later, the conquests of the Almoravides are wrested from them by other arrivals from Africa, the fanatical sect of the Almohades. Encouraged by this dissension, the Christian states for the first time send their representatives to a national assembly. The first Cortes meets at Burgos. Six years later the Christians suffer defeat, but recover themselves and inflict a heavy blow upon the Moors at the battle of Las Navas de Tolosa. It is followed by repeated hammering, extending over nearly forty years, until the Moorish power is beaten back and by the year 1251 is confined entirely to the kingdom of Granada.

Then, for the space of two hundred and forty years, there was a comparative lull. Under the enlightened rule of the Nasride dynasty the province of Granada enjoyed a prosperity that invited friendly relations even with the Christians. The wealth derived from its mines, industries and agriculture exceeded that of the ancient Caliphate of Cordova. The period represented, in fact, the Golden Age of Moorish civilization in Spain, the flower and symbol of which remains to-day, though shorn of much of its magnificence, in the still exquisite palace of the Alhambra. So skilfully by treaty and otherwise did the rulers of Granada conciliate the Christians that their reign might have been continued indefinitely, but for two causes: internal dissensions and the fixed idea of Ferdinand and Isabella to fulfil their obligations as Catholic Kings. They lived for the purpose of expelling the infidel, and the rivalry between the two great Moorish tribes, the Zegri and the Abencerrages, gave them the opportunity. It had resulted in the throne being occupied by the youthful weakling, Boabdil. He fell into the hands of Ferdinand and Isabella at the battle of Lucena, and consented to remain neutral while they attacked the coast cities of Granada. Finally they appeared before Granada itself and Boabdil, after a frantic but futile effort to oppose them, was forced into a treaty of peace, by which the city was surrendered. Ten years later the last of the Moors had been expelled from Spain or compelled to be baptised.

Before proceeding with the story it is worth while to consider the effect which this long struggle of seven hundred and eighty years had had upon the Spanish character. In the first place it had fused the nation into one; not by some sudden stroke of patriotic ardor but by a slow and painful process, in which the patriotism had been tested in the forge of adversity, stiffened and tempered on the anvil of endurance and proven by long experiences. Its qualities were trenchant, uncompromising, decisively complete. The Spaniard had become a hero to himself; sufficient in and for himself; realising his superiority and wrapping it about with a mantle of haughty exclusiveness. He had learned to rely upon himself and had justified his confidence by victory, hardly won and dearly bought; he was a

Spaniard—*verbum sat*. But he had been more than patriot; he had been a Paladin of the Faith; a Knight of the Cross; a Soldier of Christendom, Champion of the Holy Catholic Church. The consciousness of this had sustained him in adversity; quickened his strength in hours of vigil, inflamed him to the attack and crowned both victories and defeats with divine glory. An intense passion of spiritual ecstasy burned within him. He was at once a man of action, hard and practical, and a pietistic dreamer, a fanatic and visionary. How this mingling of qualities affected Spanish art, causing it, on the one hand, to be distinctively national and, on the other, a product of naturalistic method and highly pietistic motive will appear in the course of our story.

. . . .

It was, perhaps, Spain's misfortune that her victories over the Moors were not succeeded by a period of settled conditions. For already she had entered upon a career of brilliant enterprise in the arts of peace. Under the patronage of Queen Isabella and of prelates, such as Cardinal Ximenes de Cisneros, Archbishop of Toledo, whose power rivaled that of the Crown, great architectural works were inaugurated and sculptors and painters were drawn from Flanders and Germany to decorate them. Learning was still further encouraged by the founding of a new University at Alcalá de Henares to supplement the famous foundation of Salamanca, and men of letters and artists were welcomed and honored at Court. Among them stand out the names of Pulgar, the first historian of Castile; Cota, the first Spanish dramatist and Rincon, the earliest of the native painters. The sixteenth century, in fact, opened with a brilliant dawn, full of promise for the new nation, if only it might have had leisure to consolidate and develop naturally its resources. But it was drawn almost immediately into the whirl of foreign conquests.

On the one hand it became involved in the affairs of the kingdom of Naples, which was conquered by the Spanish general, Gonsalvo de Cordova; on the other hand, by the bull of the Spanish Borgia Pope, Alexander VI, it was put in possession of all the conquests it might make in the New World. In both cases the immediate results may possibly be considered a boon, but they were followed by consequences disastrous to the nation and the Spanish character. The occupation of Naples brought the country in touch with Italian civilization, then approaching its zenith, but flung it into the vortex of European intrigue and warfare. Wealth began to flow in from the Americas, but at the expense of national demoralization. The conquest of inferior nations, inferiorly equipped with arms of offense and defense, may easily result in cruelty and the general sapping of the truly soldier spirit, while the lust of gold which soon began to inspire it converted these champions of the Faith into brutal buccaneers and plunderers. Further, it sapped the energies of the nation at home. For, why laboriously develop the resources of the country, when a stream of wealth was flowing into it from abroad? National progress, therefore, was checked and in time stifled; while the incoming wealth soon began to go out in prodigal expenditure over useless European wars. It became a mad gamble in which the spiritual qualities of the Spanish character were overwhelmed with the intoxication of power, while its exclusiveness and pride blinded the nation to the inevitable catastrophe.

A fact antecedent to all these causes of national deterioration was that even before the conquest of Granada the Catholic Sovereigns had established the Inquisition. With this devilish engine, operated in the name of God and the Catholic Faith, the Spaniard attempted to check the progress of Europe and effectively crushed his own. In time he expelled from the Peninsula the Jews, who in Spain had been among the foremost in learning and industrial energy; the Moors and finally the Morescoes, the progeny of the Christianised Moors and Spaniards, who had perpetuated the crafts in which the Moors had been so skilled. Enterprise was thus banished and Spain deliberately committed herself to the part of a reactionary against progress. In time England and Holland wrested from her her resources in the New World. She shrank within the limits of her own Peninsula, which had been already drained of initiation and productivity. In time, all that became left to her of her proud possessions was the dogmatic form of the Catholic religion. It had ceased to be spiritual inspiration and passed into a phase of sentimentalism, whence it dwindled to a mere formalism, existing amid irreligion and moral degradation.

. . . .

In the last sentence we have anticipated the national prostration of the eighteenth century, following upon the exhaustion of the previous one. It remains to summarise the events which intervened. Ferdinand and Isabella were succeeded by their grandson, Charles I of Spain, better known as the Emperor Charles V of Germany. He was the son of their daughter, Joanna, who had been married to the Archduke Philip of Austria, son of Emperor Maximilian of Germany. Thus Charles brought Spain under the rule of the great Hapsburg family, which even to the present time has provided monarchs for Germany and Austria. Joanna died insane, and the taint of her disease clung to her descendants. Born in Ghent in 1500 and educated in Flanders, Charles I at the death of his father in 1506 inherited the Netherlands. On the death of Ferdinand in 1516 he became King of Spain, and in 1519 was elected Emperor of Germany, the defeated competitor being Francis I of France. The rivalry between these two led to a protracted war, fought out chiefly in Italy, on the possession of which each had fastened his ambition. Francis was made captive at the battle of

Pavia in 1527 and forced into a treaty of peace; but the war was renewed two years later and Charles' troops under the renegade Frenchman, Constable of Bourbon, entered Rome and sacked it, taking the Pope prisoner. This, however, was but an incident in the political game, for Charles, as became a grandson of the Catholic Kings, was a staunch Defender of the Faith, and endeavored to impose it upon his Protestant subjects in Germany and the Netherlands. For the good of their souls he subjected them to the ravages of war and the horrors of the Inquisition, and for the filling of his military chest mulcted them by fines as well as taxation. Then at the age of fifty-five, exhausted in mind and body by his heroic exertions on behalf of Catholicism and his own ambitions, and by his various forms of self-indulgence, he handed over the Imperial Crown to his brother, Ferdinand, and the Kingdom of Spain and his "dear Netherlands" to his son, Philip. He himself, under the plea of caring for his soul's welfare, retired to the monastery of San Juste, whence he continued to meddle with affairs of State, meanwhile surfeiting his appetites and making a collection of clocks and watches. His bedroom commanded a view of the High Altar of the Church and was decorated with Titian's *Gloria*, in which picture the artist has represented the ex-Emperor in a white robe, welcomed by the Virgin at the throne of God; while his hopeful son, Philip, is among the mortals who gaze up devoutly at the imperial apotheosis.

Alas! for Philip; he had the doggedness but not the genius of his father. Meanwhile the times were changing, and he did not know it. Despotism, whether religious or political, no longer was to go unquestioned. What the Netherlands had endured from Charles they refused to submit to from his son. The more so that, while his father had chastised them with whips, he, in the person of the unspeakable Alva, chastised them with scorpions. The United Provinces revolted and the rest of Philip's life was spent in a vain effort to crush the Dutch patriots and the English who had more or less espoused their cause. Meanwhile the fleets of both countries were sweeping the Spaniards from the high seas. When Philip died in 1598, he left to his son, Philip III, the legacy of a fruitless foreign war, a ruined commerce, and an impoverished treasury. As an enduring monument of himself he left the Escoriál.

The decline of Spanish prestige and prosperity was accelerated by Philip III, an easy-going person, who even refused to take any active part in the selection of his own wife. He languidly continued the embellishment of the palaces which his father had built, and posed mildly as a patron of the arts. Under his feeble rule the power of the crown declined, while that of the nobility correspondingly increased; and to them probably more than to the king himself must be attributed the crime and economical blunder of the final expulsion of the Morescoes. An adventitious lustre is added to the reign of this king and his father by the genius of Cervantes, Lope de Vega, the dramatist, and the great artist, El Greco.

Succeeding to the crown at the age of seventeen, Philip IV resigned the government to his favorite and prime-minister, the Count-Duke Olivares, whose idea of statesmanship was to keep his royal master as far as possible in ignorance of the impending ruin of the kingdom. To this end he renewed the war in Holland, which had been interrupted by a twelve years' truce, and, with no decisive result except the squandering of revenue, prolonged it until the final recognition of Dutch Independence in 1648. Over eighty years had been expended in endeavoring to set back the clock to the principles and methods of the Middle Ages and in the process the proud empire, inaugurated by the Catholic Kings, Ferdinand and Isabella, had been drained of its vitality. The colonial possessions began to fall one by one into the hands of foreigners and Spain herself was enfeebled and demoralised. Meanwhile Philip played the part of a Maecenas in what proved to be the Golden Age of Spanish literature and art.

Among the names which gave a lustre to the Court were the veteran Lope de Vega; Calderon, author among other dramas of the "Comedies of Cape and Sword"; Velez de Guevara, playwright and novelist, whose "El Diablo Cojuelo" was the original of Le Sage's "Le Diable Boiteux"; Luis de Gongora, the poet; Quevedo, the satirist; Bartolomé Argensola, historian, and Antonio de Solis, poet, dramatist and author of "The History of the Conquest of Mexico." Philip himself posed, with considerable warrant, as a poet and musician, and even took part as an actor in the musical and dramatic entertainments which

THE CATHOLIC KINGS SCHOOL OF CASTILE
AT PRAYER XV CENTURY

THE PRADO

enlivened the ennui of the Court in the palace of Buen Retiro. He was also, as an amateur, skilful in drawing and painting. This doubtless helped him to appreciate the merits of Velasquez, who to the world outside of Spain represents the subject of most significance in his life. Philip's companionship with the artist, five years his elder, which except for the brief intervals in which one or the other of them was traveling, lasted for thirty-seven years, indeed until Velasquez' death, is the one thing on which the student of history and of art cares to dwell. It has secured for Philip IV a recognition which his political importance would have denied him.

The increasing impotence of the Hapsburg family of Spanish king's reached its climax in Philip's son, Charles II. One has but to glance at the latter's portrait, painted by Juan Carreño, to realise the physical and mental degeneracy that the family type has undergone. The type, as one sees it in Titian's equestrian portrait of his great-great-grandfather, Charles I of Spain and V of Germany, is already abnormal. The grey eyes, for all their sternness and penetrating character, have a pathetic cast of melancholy; the under jaw protrudes like that of an ape. But the chin is massive, as indicative of force as of ferocity. In Philip II, as he appears in Titian's portrait in the Prado, the face has lengthened; the eyes have lost their piercing gaze, and while no less melancholy, have an expression of deliberate cruelty. The coarseness of the lower part of the face is displayed in the exaggerated sensuality of the out-turned lower lip, beneath which is a tapering chin, that has a suggestion of blended weakness and petty doggedness. In the equestrian portrait of Philip III, which is supposed to have been painted by Bartolomé Gonzáles and effectively retouched by Velasquez, the monarch's head is carried a little back, a gesture which extenuates with probable intention the protrusion of the lower part. But the chin is feebly pointed, the under lip pendulous, while the eye suggests an empty vacuity, that is echoed in the mild fierceness of the upcurling moustache. It is a face vain, stupid and not a little commonplace. The last quality, at least, is absent, from the portraits of Philip IV. The face, especially when young, reflects the King's intrinsic refinement; but its length has become exaggerated, the protruding under-lip and jaw are puffed and fleshy, weakly sensual, while the eyes are apathetic. The expression of the whole is of a nature nearly worn out, that can only be stirred to occasional alertness by the stimulant of trivial excitements. Finally, in Carreño's portrait of Charles II, (p. 132) appears a total extinction of active faculties, soft sensuousness rather than sensuality, a settled look of apathy and the profound depression of a religious monomaniac.

Charles was scarcely four years old when the death of his father in 1665 made him king of a bankrupt country. It was the policy of the Queen Mother, whose regency was marked by political incompetence and personal amours, to keep her son as childish as possible. And, when he reached his majority at the age of fifteen and supplanted his mother's influence by that of Don Juan of Austria, the latter also schemed to keep his master in a condition of mental darkness and dependence. Thus Charles was the victim alike of racial degeneracy and of thwarted development. Complete incapacity to govern himself or others was the natural result. He shunned the affairs of state, mildly supported the arts as far as the beggared state of the treasury would permit, and sank into a religious mania that found satisfaction in attending auto-da-fés and prostrating himself in acts of personal penance. Dying childless in 1700, he brought the Hapsburg line to an inglorious conclusion; and the succession passed to a branch of the Bourbon family.

The Crown was offered by the Spanish people to Philip, grandson of Louis XIV. He was the nephew of the late king, being the son of Philip

IV's daughter, Maria Theresa, and Louis XIV. When, however, this marriage was made Louis had expressly renounced all claims to the Spanish throne, both on his own behalf and that of his heirs; and the renunciation had been confirmed by the Cortes. Meanwhile, another sister of Charles II had been married to Leopold, Emperor of Germany. She also had renounced her claim to the Spanish Crown, but the understanding had not been ratified by the Cortes. This afforded a pretext for the Elector of Bavaria, who had married her daughter, to claim the succession in opposition to Philip. A third claimant had been the Emperor Leopold himself, who however, waived his rights in favor of his second son, the Archduke Charles. The dispute had been in progress during the late king's life, and Louis XIV had made a treaty with England and Holland, recognising the claims of the Elector of Bavaria. When, however, the crown was offered to Philip and accepted on his behalf by Louis XIV, England and Holland made a coalition with Austria and Germany to compel the recognition of the Archduke Charles. Hence the thirteen years' war of the Spanish succession, in which Marlborough gained a series of victories over the French and Bavarians, the Archduke ravaged the Peninsula, and the English and Dutch fleets preyed on Spanish commerce and captured Gibraltar. Finally, by the Treaty of Utrecht in 1714 the succession of Philip V was ratified.

He had been brought up by Louis XIV to be undesirous and incapable of taking part in political affairs. While the country continued to be involved in disastrous foreign wars this *roi fainéant* amused himself with building a summer palace and laying out gardens, both in the French style. He also imported the French portrait-painter, Van Loo. It must be added, however, that the stock of Spanish painters had been exhausted. Native art, indeed, for the time, was all but dead. It so remained through the thirteen years' reign of his son, Ferdinand VI, though he tried to galvanize it into official life by inaugurating the Academy of San Fernando. This king was succeeded by his brother Charles III, who had already distinguished himself by his wise rule of the Kingdom of the Two Sicilies. His portrait by Goya, in the costume of a sportsman, shows him to be a man of awkward build and of homely, though kind and shrewd, face. He proved himself a generous patron of second-rate artists, inviting the German painter, Raphael Mengs and the Venetian, Tiepolo, to his Court; built the present gallery of the Prado and issued an order forbidding the exportation of paintings by the great masters of Spain. He appears to have had some inkling of the genius of Goya, who, however, did not come into prominence until the succession of Charles IV.

Charles IV was an amiable imbecile and his Queen, Maria Luisa, the shameless subject of notorious scandal. One of her favorites, Manuel

Godoy, advanced from the rank and file of a regiment of the Guards to the title of Duke of Alcudia, was entrusted with the duties of prime minister. After embroiling the country in successive wars with France and England, he finally attached himself to the cause of Napoleon and favored the latter's design to place his brother Joseph on the Spanish throne. The French entered Spain in 1808 and compelled Charles to abdicate. But in the same year the Spaniards rose against the invaders, and the English came to their assistance. Then followed the Peninsular War, during which Wellington gradually expelled the French troops, but not until they had pillaged the cathedrals and churches and carried off a large number of the finest works of art. For Marshal Soult, with the predatory instincts of an unscrupulous dealer, sent his emissaries ahead of the army. Armed with the "Dictionary of Painters and Paintings" by Cean Bermudez, they identified and attached the most famous canvases, which the Marshal compelled their owners to part with at his own terms. On the conclusion of the war many of these were returned to Spain under the terms of the treaty of peace, but a number of masterpieces had already passed through Soult's rapacious hands into the public and private galleries of Europe.

This treaty of peace, which restored the Throne to Charles' son, Ferdinand VII, is the end of the history of Spain so far as it concerns the growth and development and decline of her national art. She has had painters of repute since 1814; but not in sufficient numbers to constitute a school or even a noticeable artistic movement. Under weak and constantly changing governments, controlled by the Church and existing mainly for taxation, her arts, like her commerce and industries dwindled to an almost negligible condition, from which only recently there are indications of recovery.

CHAPTER II

CHARACTERISTICS OF SPANISH PAINTING

SPANISH Painting, so far as it represents a school, is singularly limited in scope and rigidly circumscribed. This is due partly to the racial character, self-centered and conservative, out of which it grew: partly also, to the influences that immediately shaped its growth. For it developed under the patronage of the Crown and the Church. Nor were these, in theory or in practice, antagonistic to each other. The Church was the embodiment, the Crown the defender, of the Faith: the efforts of both being united to preserve the Faith against the inroads alike of Humanism and Protestantism. Hence the art of Spain, while it might be incidently concerned with portraiture, discovered its essential characteristics as the exponent of Bible story and Saintly lore and as an exhortation to faith and pious living. Its home was the sacred edifice, where it embellished walls, vaultings, and ceilings, or presided in the ceremonial altar-piece. Its language for the most part was that of the vernacular; the sacred imagery being translated into the idiom of common knowledge, its mysteries into expressions of common experience. It was in consequence a naturalistic art.

Had the artists of Spain painted for the general public or followed their own bent in the pursuit of beauty, they would doubtless have developed branches of genre and still life painting that might have emulated the work of the Holland artists; for they had a similar love of the intimate beauty of simple things around them. But since they had to reach the masses of the people through the intervention mostly of the Church, which not only commissioned the subject but prescribed its treatment, they achieved their self-expression through religious pictures which had the character of sacred genre. Yet this Spanish brand of genre is inferior to the secular genre of Holland or to the sacred genre of old Flemish religious paintings. It has a quality, perceptible in neither of the latter, of obviousness. Its motive is less surely an æsthetic delight in things of beauty; more evidently influenced by the practical intention of rounding out the story.

I doubt if the student of Spanish painting, particularly if he visits Spain, can escape the feeling that it exhibits a certain oppressive obviousness. How is this to be accounted for? In the first place, surely, by the influence of the Church, ever more intent on making art a handmaid of its own purposes than on developing its own inherent beauties. And, if this was true under the conditions in Italy, where the Church itself was penetrated with Humanism, how much more is it to be expected under those which existed in Spain! But there is another reason, incident to the Spanish character. The latter, as has been suggested in the previous chapter, was the product of a long and heroic struggle on behalf of nationality and the Christian Faith. Among its conspicuous traits, in consequence, were self-consciousness and inflated egoism; traits that, if you consider it, are those of the actor; the necessary groundwork on which he builds his better qualities as an artist.

The Spaniards are a race of actors. The arts in which they have most naturally expressed themselves are those of the drama and the novel of character and action. And this trait similarly affects their painting. It is dramatic, concerned frequently with action, always with characterisation. Meanwhile, self-consciousness and egoism readily yield to the temptation of exaggeration. Spanish literature evaded this weakness because it was left to go its own way and the artistic conscience of the author was permitted to discover for itself a sense of true values. But in the painter's case the Church intervened and being, so to say, interested in the box-office receipts, compelled him to play to the gallery. It favored sensationalism and encouraged melodrama. The meekness of the martyr must be represented so that the dullest spectator would not miss the moral; the executioner's hatred of virtue so portrayed that no one could fail to recognise him as a villain; love and devotion must be sentimentalised, and blood, pain and disease so vividly exhibited that the crudest sensibilities would be wrung. Imagination must not be counted upon and suggestion, the subtle road thereto, must be abandoned for the direct and detailed statement. Aim at the crude instincts and make the message obvious!

This Spanish tendency toward the related traits of exaggeration and obviousness is not confined to painting. It appears also in the architecture and sculpture. Foreign architects, for example, were employed in the erection of cathedrals in the Gothic style; but the latter's noble logic of plan and elevation was disturbed by the innovations which Spanish taste, or lack of it, dictated. Conspicuous among these was the erection of a Coro in the center of the nave; an inclosure walled around, carried to a great height and profusely adorned with sculpturesque ornament. This monstrous choir effectually blocks the view of the high-altar from any spot except the narrow space which separates the two, and also interrupts what should be one of the sublime features of a Gothic cathedral, its endless variety of stately vistas. In every direction the perspective of pillars, arches and vaultings is barred by the tasteless magnificence of the Coro. For the latter, like the Capilla Mayor with its high-altar, is overloaded with excess of ornament. In one case it may be in the "plateresque" style, a network of intricate and minute embellishments that vies with the dainty exuberance of the workers in silver-plate. Elsewhere, it is wantonly "grotesque" or pompously "baroque" or characterised by that orgy of material extravagance, called "Churrigueresque" after the name of the sculptor who introduced it. In this, sculpture has been degraded to the most blatant naturalism; Madonnas clothed like dolls in brocaded gowns; the tragedy of Calvary or the glory of Heaven, presented with figures, background and accessories, painted, posed and set like a theatrical tableau. It is not for a moment suggested that there is no beauty and grandeur in Spanish architecture and sculpture. Yet to one whose taste is attuned to the imaginative spaciousness, sublimity and mystery of pure Gothic or to the inventive refinement of choice Renaissance design, the net impression of a Spanish cathedral is likely to be one of oppression and distaste. And more so, as one analyses the psychological cause of this extravagant display. It seems to be the Spanish instinct to close himself round with interest in what is nearest to him, so that he abandons breadth or height of vision—imagination, in fact—in favor of the immediately present, which he invests with all the fervor of his pent up nature. This leads inevitably to a materialistic point of view and to the baldly naturalistic method; in a word, to the obviousness which we have noted.

Spain, in fact, with its large admixture of Germanic blood, exhibits in its art the trait that affects other races akin to the Teutonic: the German itself, the English and American. She, no more than they, has much sense of beauty in the abstract. The idea that beauty for its own sake is desirable may penetrate the imagination of some artists in all these countries, but is a principle of art in none of them, and by the general public of all is not understood. The usual idea is that painting is primarily the representation of some person, place or thing, and is to be judged by what it represents. The idea that it should contribute to the beauty of life, and that beauty is one of the qualities most needful and desirable in life; that, indeed, properly considered, it should be the ideal of life, is even to-day only slowly dawning upon our comprehension. We still make the ideal of our civilization material progress and the ideal of education the preparation to play a part in it. In a word, our ideal is materialistic; a contradiction of terms, confusing the high issues of life. For, if a man or a nation is to have an ideal it must be something above the necessary matter of life, correlating the spiritual sense to what it conceives of spirit in the universe. It was so that the Greek, learning of Egypt and the Orient, drawing inspiration, in fact, from the deep wells of human consciousness, established his ideal and interpreted it under the symbol of beauty.

For my own part, this difference between the older idea of art and our own, which was shared by Spain, is most illuminatively enforced by the contrast between two of the great architectural monuments of Spain: the

Escoriál and the Alhambra. Both are palaces, memorials of the greatest epoch in the history of each race; but one is a palace of the dead and of preparation for death, the other a lordly pleasure house, redolent of the joy of living; the Escoriál is a monument of sternness; the Alhambra a miracle of beauty.

Yet for the student of humanity and of art in relation thereto what a poignant interest attaches to the Escoriál! True, it is the self-expression of one man; but the imagination may not be astray in discovering in it some expression also of the race and its time. For Philip II was so loyal a son of the Church or, if you will, so morbid a victim of the Church's influence, and that influence was then so rooted in the conscience of the

S. URSULA   SPANISH SCHOOL, XV CENTURY

THE PRADO

people, that he was in a large measure representative of them.

Philip was bound by the terms of his inheritance to create a mausoleum for the remains of his father, Charles V. He set about making it a burying place of sufficient dignity for his father, himself and succeeding Catholic Kings. To the mausoleum must be attached a church, and to the latter a monastery, to make perpetual provision for the saying of masses. His father had retired to a monastery after laying down the cares of government. Philip, while still handling the affairs of his vast dominion, would also lead the cloistered life. Meanwhile there were the mundane needs of a court to be considered and Philip himself tempered his asceticism with gallantry, so that a palace must be included. Hence ensued the idea of the Escoriál, wherein life consorts with death and business and pleasure are pursued under the shadow of a judgment to come. Surely a monument to the strangest medley of motives that history can show! Morbid, magnificent!

Architects were employed, but Philip constantly supervised the design. He planned his monument to last forever. Far from the possible vicissitudes of the capital, remote from the petty changes of daily life, he laid its foundations in the bed-rock of the mountains; and built their strength into its walls. With its back to the precipitous wall of the Guadarrama Sierra, it stands a colossal squared mass, facing the undulating vista of tableland. Its facades are severely simple, bare of ornamental detail, proclaiming their monastic purpose; and similarly the interior, as originally planned, was characterised by the dignity of constructional simplicity. The church also, until Luca Giordano at a later period covered the vaultings with flaunting mural paintings, was a unique example of stern austerity; its plan of a Greek cross being uninterrupted by a central coro and the only magnificence permitted being massed about the high-altar. A strange contrast, in fact, the imagination of Philip offered to the art instincts of his people. While they eschewed vistas and rejoiced in extravagance of detail, he was wedded to simplicity and sought a prospect of the widest vision. Yet in his personal life he shrank into narrowness. A private door communicated with a corner seat at the back of the coro, so that unobserved he could join the monks, as one of them, in their devotional routine. While he provided himself with a palace for ceremonial purposes, he actually lived in a tiny suite of meagre rooms, sleeping in a cubicle. Its window opened into the church, commanding a view of the high-altar, where the celebrant as he said mass stood directly above the tombs of the dead kings. This Pantheon of the dead, a low, octagonal chamber with flattened vaultings, lined with shelves on which repose sarcophagi, was originally of extreme simplicity. For the present bastard profusion of sombre ornamentation was added by Philips III and IV.

To-day as one wanders through this vast and silent edifice of the Escoriál it can well seem as if that sanctuary of death, buried beneath the church, is the dead heart, connected by the arteries of its nearly one hundred miles of corridors with the huge organs and spreading limbs of a prodigious leviathan. One has left behind the exhilaration of the air of the Sierras the glorious spaciousness of the outside prospect, and as the artificial vastness closes in about one, the spirit becomes numbed and chill. It is a stupendous Golgotha, a colossal Place of Skulls. Yet we shall be lacking in imagination if we cannot realise that the dead heart once beat and that the ponderous body once enshrined a soul. It may have been a mad soul; certainly it was a proud one, of high exaltation, white to its core with the flame of an intense ideal. None the less was it something of a craven soul, evading the problems of this life, and fearing the life to come; closing its eyes to the light and wrapping itself in the darkness of superstition. It is the soul of one man that was thus enshrined; but in many respects it is revealed as the soul of the Spanish people.

Seen at noonday in summer, the Escoriál stands, shadowless in the sunshine, at the foot of the bare Sierra, looking out over a vista of barren stubble, parched grass and dried up water-courses; an undulating sweep of pallid buff, interrupted sparsely by grey olive bushes; pitilessly inhospitable. But, in the slanting light of the afternoon, the Sierras near and far lose the bleakness of their pinkish buff beneath transparent tones of mauve and lavender, while the harsh nudity of the endless vega becomes clothed in tender veils of variously modulated greys. Even the inexorableness of the granite pile is assuaged, as the shadows creep about its base, the contours and surfaces of its facades melt into iridescent hues and the dome and towers rise up to meet the cooling sky with something of aerial suggestion. Slowly, as the light wanes the Escoriál and its vast setting become to the imagination spiritualised; but the spirit that hovers over them and enters into yours is, if I mistake not, for all its beauty impregnated with sadness, which, as the darkness blots out distance and buries the monastery beneath the gloom of the Sierras, dies into a sense of awe.

And now let us revisit the Alhambra, which enshrines the soul of another race. No colossal formality here, or precision of foot-rule and compass from which the free spirit of the artist's imagination has been dogmatically barred! On the contrary, the palace of the Moorish kings grew cell to cell by accretion, expressive of an accumulating sense of the power and joy of life, alive with the breath of artistic imagination. It dominates its own hill, looking across, on the one hand, to the protecting barrier of higher hills, and on the other, over a smiling hospitable vega, a far reaching garden of luxuriant fertility. The hill itself is a paradise of refreshment. Its slopes are richly clothed with shade trees and semi-tropical vegetation, embowered in flowers, fragrant with the scents of living growths, musical with the song of birds, the tinkle of tiny runnels, and the plash of fountains and cascades. Set above this scene of ordered wildness, where the license of nature is united to the task of man, stands what is left of the palace of the Arab Sovereigns of Granada.

There is no need to describe its plan of gardens, fountains, courts and corridors, halls of ceremony and suites of living rooms. It is the spirit of the whole that we may try to capture. Here, as in the Mosque of Cordova, the Arab's love of vistas is revealed; but while the former spreads over a large space, the perspectives of the Alhambra are actually restricted. In their case even more than in the other is created an illusion of distance. The triumph is one not of material emphasis but of artistic suggestion. It was the human imagination, finding its free expression in art, that gave form and fabric to this Oriental dream of beauty. It is a visualised symphony, whose theme is life; the joy of life and beauty that irradiates the joy. And the inspiration is drawn from nature. To those who know the Alhambra it will not sound like freakishness of speech to say, that the imagination of the artist has ensnared a portion of the spirit of beauty which roams at large in the desert and sky and lurks in the silences of woods and gardens; and, because he felt the phenomena of nature in relation to the supreme whole, has captured something of the infinity of the universal and enshrined it in his microcosm of beauty. Also more intimately he has fashioned his invention upon nature; studying her forms and methods and adapting them to the conventions of art. In the endless variety of decorative encrustration with which the wall-spaces, the soffits of the arches and the vaultings of the chambers are embroidered, the motives are drawn from the interlacing of boughs and vines, the rhythm of the brooklet meandering through luxuriant undergrowth of vines and flowers, from the facets of the crystal and the accumulated cells of bees. But they are not interpreted in a naturalistic vein. The Oriental imagination, at its best, rises above naturalistic representation; it accepts the fertilization of nature, but conventionalises the product to conform to the artist's idea of abstract beauty.

It may be that in the Alhambra he has carried this idealization too far and become too prodigal with its motives. The dainty fabric has little structural dignity; architectonic substance being sacrificed to vistas and surface decoration, while the last may easily be judged too profuse. Yet the Arab, when he chose, was a builder and engineer, continuing the Roman tradition of solid and scientific construction. Even at the Alhambra this fact is attested by the foundations that are rooted in the rock and carried down its precipitous flank, and by the aqueducts which convey water from the neighboring hills to supply the fountains and baths, the sudorific chambers and the system of heating. He faced the necessities and facts of life as they arose, but in the pleasure-house of his soul surrendered himself to the abstract, wrapping himself in contemplation of the beautiful. So he encouraged his artists until their imagination reached its zenith of profuse invention in the so-called "Room of the Two Sisters."

Above a dado of iridescent glass mosaic the walls are overlaid with a rich lace work as of carved ivory, the interstices of which are colored red and blue. Their surfaces are interrupted by niches, framed with columns and arches of surpassing delicacy. From the four corners, at considerable height project pendentives, converting the square of the room into an octagon from

THE APPARITION OF
THE VIRGIN
TO BERNARDINE
MONKS

? PEDRO
BERRUGUETE

THE PRADO

which springs the domed ceiling. The pendentives are groups of stalactite forms, and the vaulting above is composed of innumerable concave cells. Each differing slightly from the others, they cling together in pendent masses, here projecting like a bunch of swarming bees, there receding into the mystery of a fairy grotto; all the while mounting up the curve of the ceiling, which undulates like a vine yielding to the weight of its grapes; climbing higher and higher in endless frolic of invention until they draw together at the ceiling's peak. Enough gold still adheres to the myriad facets to suggest to the imagination the mysterious lustre of the ceiling, when it was lighted by a suspended lantern with its clusters of crystal lights. This gem of the Alhambra jewel, the heart of the Harem chambers, opens, as you remember, on one side into an alcove. Through the windows of this appear the tops of cypress trees, which rise from the boskage of pomegranates, roses and oleanders in a little garden court. On the other side, the "Court of the Lions," once shaded with orange trees, still soothes the ear with the plash of its central fountain and the drip of the tiny jets that spring like rods of silver from the marble pavement of the arcades. A spot, indeed of exquisite sensations; where everything conspires to alternate moods of reverie and poignant stimulation; where the physical senses are rarified, exalted, till perception swims into a sea of subtleties that melts into a dreamy subconsciousness of infinity.

This you may say is a supreme achievement, tainted with weakness. Here the yearning after beauty for its own sake has created such a subtlety and luxuriance of beauty as to suggest that the motive was ornament for the sake of ornament; sense-gratification for indulgence sake; exquisiteness at the cost of living energy. For, while the maze of decoration is ordered with most refined sensibility, it is none the less expressive of inordinate and almost tortured sensuousness. If you adopt this view it is to admit that the Alhambra was a product of the decadence of the Oriental idea; and it is interesting to note how it bred a corresponding decadence in the artistic motives of the Christian conquerors. It was unquestionably from the Arabs that the Spaniard derived his taste for excess. But his racial instinct and his Catholic faith colored the result with a great difference. His sensuous and religious ecstasy found their expression not in abstract symbols but in concrete actualities. They prompted him to take delight in the actual representation of blood and torture and to render his conception of Heaven by means of sculptured figures reposing on marble clouds amid gilded spikes of glory. Gradually, in fact, he degraded his conception to the most obvious kind of perception. He expressed his spiritual ideas in terms of naturalism.

It may seem illogical to invite the reader to be interested in Spanish art and then discourage him by laying bare its weakness. But I believe that every one who visits Spain, where alone the inwardness of Spanish art can be reached, must feel at the outset more or less conscious of these limitations to his interest; that, in fact, he suffers a preliminary discouragement. If so, is it not better to admit it; to accustom oneself to the expectation of temporary disillusionment, in order that one may the sooner get over it and settle down to a just appreciation of the admirable qualities which actually exist in Spanish painting?

CHAPTER III

A PANORAMIC VIEW

Part I: To the End of the Sixteenth Century.

TO the student who is in pursuit of æsthetic enjoyment rather than critical research the art of Spain resolves itself into the works of a comparatively small number of painters. It is these who are represented in the galleries of Europe and America and form the chief attraction in the Prado and smaller museums of Spain, as well as in the cathedrals and churches; at least in those cases, not too frequent, where there is sufficient light to see them. The spell exercised by these artists each in his different way, is so arresting that one may easily be indifferent to those of minor quality. On the other hand, our interest is increased if we glance over the whole field, the level of which is interrupted by conspicuous individuals, and thus view the latter in their respective times and places in the general story.

It must not be forgotten that the racial characteristics of Spain and her art, while they preserve a general national uniformity, were modified by the circumstances of different environments. Even before their union by the marriage of Ferdinand and Isabella, the kingdoms of Castile and Aragón presented a noted difference. The former included besides the province of Castile, the other divisions of territory in the northwest of the Peninsula; while Aragón embraced Catalonia and Valencia, the provinces bordering on the Mediterranean, and had extended her authority to the Balearic Isles, Sardinia and Sicily. The geographical distribution tells its own tale: Castile, with her bleak Sierras and wind-swept, sun-parched plains, a region of strenuousness; Aragón, dipping her hot feet in the Mediterranean, her asperities assuaged by influences from over-sea. For, while Castile was early disposed to derive her foreign influences from the Netherlands and Germany, Aragón and especially Valencia drew theirs from Italy. Later, when the union of the entire country was achieved by the conquest of Andalusia and Granada, the climatic conditions of these two provinces and their proximity to the Mediterranean naturally drew them into close relations both with Valencia and Italy. It remains only to mention in the way of anticipation, that the seat of Government, being always in Castile and finally established in Madrid, became a nucleus to which the various influences from other parts of the country were attracted. Thus, while the Schools of Valencia and Andalusia preserved their local characteristics, the

School of Castile, which later is more specifically known as the School of Madrid, became under the patronage of the Court more cosmopolitan.

The sources of painting in Spain, as in other countries, are to be looked for, first in illuminated manuscripts and secondly in the remains of mural decorations. The earliest examples of the latter are to be found in the figures of saints which adorn the little church of El Cristo de la Luz in Toledo and in some scenes from the Passion on the vaulting of the chapel of St. Catherine in San Isidoro in Léon. These are attributed to the twelfth century. Later examples of the fourteenth century, exist in Seville, in San Lorenzo, San Ildefonso and the Capella de la Antigua in the Cathedral. The subject of each is the Virgin. In the cathedral, for example, she is represented against a gold diapered background, her robe also being adorned with arabesques of gold. In her right hand she holds a rose and with her left supports the Child, while two angels suspend a crown over her head. The figure of the Father Almighty, rather small in scale, appears above. The flesh is scarcely modeled, and in the case of the Virgin is very tenderly expressed; the draperies, on the other hand, suggesting in their flatness and breadth of treatment a sense of bigness. The influence is clearly Italian and seems to present a union of the feeling of Cimabue and Fra Angelico.

It is with the beginning of the fifteenth century that one reaches sure ground. In 1428, during the reign of Juan II of Castile, the great Flemish painter, Jan Van Eyck, while on a mission to Portugal visited Madrid. His coming aroused in the Spaniards an interest in Flemish art, which resulted in the importation of paintings by Memlinc, Roger van der Weyden, Dierick Bouts, Mabuse and Patinir. The effect of their influence can be studied in the basement galleries of the Prado, where hang anonymous works by painters of the School of Castile during the fifteenth century. A very interesting series of scenes from the life of the Virgin (numbered 2178-2183) exhibits in the angular folds of the draperies and in the architecture a notable Gothic feeling, and have much of the freedom of composition and intensity of sentiment of Van der Weyden. On the other hand in No. 2184, *The Catholic Kings with their Families at Prayer Before the Virgin* reproduced on page 18, the influence of Memlinc and his period of Flemish art appears. One notes the charming glimpses of landscape, seen through the windows; the almost childlike sweetness of the faces and the truly Flemish love of beautiful detail. This is exhibited in the Virgin's crimson robe and the rosy-purple gown of the King, both of which are brocaded with designs in raised gold, and in the various accessories, particularly the church in the hand of S. Thomas Aquinas, the lily in that of S. Domingo de Guzman, and the richly decorated throne. On the back of this are curious little impish figures, that recall the weirdly whimsical inventions of Hieronymus Bosch, whose pictures, as later those of his imitator, Peeter Brueghel, were very popular in northern Spain. The figure, kneeling behind the King, is the Inquisitor-General, Tomas de Torquemada; the one behind the Queen represents S. Peter Martyr of Verona.

Ascribed to the end of the fifteenth century is the curiously interesting *S. Ursula*, reproduced on page 31. The picture forms one of a series of three, of which the first is *The Coronation of the Virgin* and the third *The Temptation of S. Anthony*. Escorted by the Pope and by bishops and cardinals, S. Ursula is seen at the head of the procession of eleven thousand virgins who are following her to Rome; but, if the legend is to be believed, will be slaughtered by the Huns near Cologne. With another example, reproduced on page 37, we reach at least the suggestion of a Spanish painter's name. *The Apparition of the Virgin to a Community of Bernardine Monks During a Ceremony of Exorcism* is ascribed, though with a query, to Pedro Berruguete. Carl Justi considers that this picture and its companions, illustrating Dominican legends, were by the Burgundian painter, Juan de Borgoña, assisted by Berruguete and another painter named Santos Cruz. To the last is attributed the traces of Peruginesque influence that occur in all the series; in the present example, in the angels surrounding the Madonna. But the chief interest lies in the varied and individual characterization which the artist has given to the heads of the monks and laity. The latter seem of Flemish type, and, if Carl Justi's attribution is correct, may, together with the architectural perspective have been executed by Juan de Borgoña. On the other hand, Berruguete was probably responsible for the monks, since they approximate to the Spanish type, as may be verified by comparing them with the character studies of this order of brotherhood by Zurbarán (see page 166).

The gradual emergence of the national type in the works of this period is again illustrated in the collection of splendid panels in the Hispanic Museum, New York. Examples 1 to 7 show the Netherlandish influence,

S. STEPHEN CONDUCTED   JUAN DE JUANES
   TO MARTYRDOM

THE PRADO

while numbers 8 and 9 represent the commencement of native feeling. Compare, for instance, the face of the woman who kneels on the left of the foreground in *S. Gregory Saying Mass* with those of the women in the high upright panel of the earlier series. The latter have a Flemish roundness of features and rather dull expression, whereas the face in the *Gregory* picture, narrows toward the chin and has something of the spiritual intensity which in the next century will be brought to its highest pitch of expression by El Greco. In fact, although Spain borrowed motives and methods from abroad, the inspiration remained her own and imprinted a native character on the product.

. . . .

This is still apparent in the art of the sixteenth century when there poured into Spain a steady flow of Italian influence. Its general tendency was to produce a number of so-called "mannerists," Spanish painters who experimented with and imitated the style of the Italian masters, particularly of the Florentines, Da Vinci, Raphael and Michelangelo. It was a necessary stage through which Spanish art had to graduate in order to acquire facility in drawing, chiaroscuro and the principles of composition. But it is not a period on which the student who is interested in art as a living expression will care to dwell. He will look upon it as probationary and merely preparatory for the later liberty of national and individual expression. Yet he may glance over it and see how even here the yeast of the national genius is fermenting the mass of borrowed and affected manners.

An example of this is afforded by the work of Juan de Juanes, one of the early names of prominence in the School of Valencia. The *S. Stephen Conducted to Martyrdom*, reproduced on page 44, is an illustration of his style. It forms one of a series, connected with the life of S. Stephen, which is now in the basement galleries of the Prado. It is not difficult to detect in these paintings the influence of Raphael. So noticeable is it, that Cean Bermudez, the chronicler of early Spanish art, assumes that Juanes must have been a pupil of the Florentine master. Subsequent research, however, has discovered that the Valencian painter was not born until 1523, three years after Raphael's death. However he may have acquired a knowledge of the latter's style, it is evident what it did for him and, through him, for the other painters of the Valencian school and the closely affiliated school of Andalusia. Comparing this picture with the earlier ones, reproduced in these pages, one observes in it a far more varied, facile and accurate skill in drawing, and that the composition, while it has lost the charm of naturalness, has gained in science. It is *organisé*, as the French say, a carefully assembled structure of inter-related parts, locked together into an ensemble. On the other hand, to anticipate the sequence of our story, this artificial unity will have to be digested before its principles can be adjusted to the naturalistic presentation which is to be the peculiar quality of Spanish art. Meanwhile we can see the naturalistic tendency already forming. The fine head, immediately behind the Saint's, is that of a Spanish gentleman of the period. All the heads, in fact, are of local types, and the exaggeration of action in the figures and of emotion in the faces, is characteristic of a nation so dramatically disposed as the Spanish, while the excess of humility in the demeanour of the Saint is characteristic of the devotional attitude of this painter toward his art. For he, like many others among the Spanish artists, is said to have painted only sacred subjects and to have prepared his spirit for the task by partaking of the Sacrament.

Another picture which helps to throw a light upon this period of Italian imitation is the *Descent from the Cross* by Pedro Campaña (page 51). This painter was born in Brussels in 1503. But, though of Flemish origin, he gained his knowledge of art in Rome, whence he passed to Spain, living in Seville for twenty-four years, until his death in 1580. Thus he was an important factor in the transitionary development of the School of Andalusia. Murillo particularly admired this picture, and at his own request was buried beneath it in the Church of Santa Cruz. When the latter was pulled down, the picture was removed to the Cathedral, where it now hangs in the Sacristy. Its indebtedness to Raphael is apparent in the group of figures at the foot of the Cross, while a Peruginesque influence is suggested in the draperies of the men upon the ladders and in the placing of their figures against the sky. But also evident is the artificiality of the whole. The gestures and expression of the women are affected; quite inadequate is the support which is being given to the Sacred Body, while the attitude of the latter is too obviously regulated with the double intention of securing certain lines in the composition and of introducing the suggestion of forgiveness of the Magdalen. In fact, the chief virtue of the picture seems to be its extremely handsome composition, which must be admitted to have great nobility as well as a fine organic simplicity. The picture, indeed, is an achievement of science; valuable for its enforcement of academic principles; yet, even so, the work, not of a master, but a manneristic imitator.

. . . .

It is with more interest than one turns to the work of another artist of this transition period, Luis de Morales. For although he experimented with various motives, his adoption of them seems to have been prompted by his search for the expression of a personally sincere religious fervor. Almost nothing is recorded of his life, beyond the few facts that he was a native of Badajoz, on the frontier of Portugal, and died there in 1586; that, except for a visit to Madrid at the invitation of Philip II he seems to have spent his life in the quiet retirement of his native city, and notwithstanding the estimation in which his pictures were held, reached an old age of poverty. For it is related that the king passing through Badajoz, sent for the artist. The latter, when as a young man he had been summoned to Court, appeared in so sumptuous an attire, that the King remonstrated with him, but was appeased by Morales' explanation that he donned it in honor of his Majesty. Now, however, he appeared in a condition of extreme destitution. To Philip's remark: "Morales, you are very old," the artist replied, "Yes, your Majesty, and very poor." The king on the spot awarded him a pension of two hundred ducats. "For your dinner," he said, to which Morales replied, "And for supper, Sire?" The King, so the story goes, accepted the jest and added another hundred ducats a year to the pension. This episode took place in 1581 and it is supposed that Morales at the time of his death, five years later, had reached the age of seventy-seven years.

Nothing is known as to the way in which Morales learned his art, but a comparative study of his various styles suggests that he may have had access to some work or copy of a work of Michelangelo, to some examples of the Milanese School of Leonardo da Vinci and to pictures of the contemporary Flemish and German Schools. The Michelangelesque influence, according to the official notice of this artist in the catalogue of the Prado Gallery, is discernible chiefly in works that are to be found in Badajoz and Lisbon. It would appear that they are distinguished by an exaggeration of manner. A similar trait appears in a *Pietá* which hangs in the Academy of San Fernando in Madrid. The Virgin is seated at the foot of the Cross, supporting the dead body of Christ. The latter is in an attitude of being seated, the arms suspended and the head laid back on the shoulder, immediately below the head of the Virgin. The nude form is as hard as if it were carved in wood, and in contrast to its pallid whiteness are long streams of crimson blood, as glossy and stiff as ribands. In fact, combined with the naturalistic correctness of the drawing the figure has an exaggerated Gothic feeling, while another excess, this time of refinement, appears in the microscopic precision with which the hair of the beard and head is represented. This delicacy, suggestive of the Milanese influence, reappears in the *Virgin Caressing the Infant Jesus* of the Prado Gallery and the variations of the same theme which may be seen in the Hispanic Museum, New York. Here, however, the meticulous rendering of the little golden chestnut curls which cluster on the heads of the Mother and Child is in accord with the loving, tender regard for refined sweetness of expression that characterises the whole treatment. The Prado also possesses an *Ecce Homo*; the figure, seen nearly to the waist, nude but for a crimson mantle which covers the shoulders and is fastened on the chest. One of the bound hands holds a reed and a crown of thorns surmounts the head, drops of blood showing on the forehead. The face, with its straight brows and deep-set eyes, long finely chiseled nose, and sensitive mouth, surrounded by a softly growing beard, the whole modeled sensitively with a Milanese subtlety of chiaroscuro, expresses an interesting blend of intellectuality and ecstasy. In this union one may easily discover an essentially Spanish feeling. However the methods may have been borrowed from elsewhere, the sentiment is Castilian of the sixteenth century, a mingling of high-bred nature and spiritual introspection.

Another picture of the Prado, selected for reproduction on page 62, is *The Presentation of the Infant Jesus in the Temple*. It is an important example, revealing a fuller capacity for ordered composition, in which there is a grandiose dignity, strangely

DESCENT FROM THE　　　　　　　　PEDRO CAMPAÑA
　　　CROSS

SEVILLE CATHEDRAL

interrupted by a littleness of feeling. The latter is particularly noticeable in the highly finished rendering of the child's body, disposed so affectedly amid the prim folds of the greyish white drapery. One may be conscious also of a certain exaggerated gesture of humility in the Virgin's figure; but, on the other hand, how firm in its assertion of liberty of action is the supple figure of the maiden who holds the basket of doves! How excellently imagined, moreover, are the spotting of the several heads, the upright lines of the candles and the broad bold spaces of the white tablecloth!

The reputation of Morales has been injured by the number of *Ecce Homos* and *Magdalens*, sentimentally mawkish, which, according to latest judgment, have been ascribed to him falsely. For, in an age of artistic copying, working for patrons who demanded an excessive display of pietistic ecstasy, he was distinguished by a considerable measure of individual temperament as well as of sincere religious feeling.

. . . .

The signal example of an individual personality, is that of Domenico Theotocopuli, popularly called El Greco from the fact that he was born in Crete. Since he will form the subject of another chapter, it is sufficient here to recall the fact that he reached Spain by way of Venice and Rome and settled in Toledo. His art bridges the last quarter of the sixteenth century and the first of the seventeenth, and, notwithstanding his foreign training, was deeply imbued with the Spanish spirit of his day.

Meanwhile, during the latter part of the sixteenth century a more direct infusion of Italian influence reached Spain through the artists whom Philip imported from Italy to decorate the Escoriál. During the first twenty-five years of his reign he had continued the patronage of Titian, commenced by his father, Charles V. The latter, after he had sat to the great Venetian, loaded him with marks of favor, including an order of nobility, and vowed that no other artist was worthy to paint Cæsar. Philip's pride equally demanded the services of the artist who was accounted the greatest of his day, and Titian was willing to give them. "Is not my aim in life," he wrote, "to refuse the services of other princes and to cling to that of your majesty?" The king's commissions were for religious subjects, but Titian, knowing the other side of his patron's nature, supplemented them with nudes and the so-called "poesies," or subjects of more or less erotic significance. Hence the collection of over forty Titian's which is one of the glories of the Prado Gallery.

Among the painters summoned from Italy by Philip II the best known are Frederico Zucchero, Pelegrino Tibaldi, Bartolomeo Carducho and Patricio Caxés. They were men of facile but inferior ability, whose work is of little interest in itself and has no part, except that of an interlude, in the development of native art. On the other hand a definite and distinguished rôle was played by the Flemish painter, Antony Mor or Moro. He had been portrait painter to Charles V in Flanders, and in 1552 came to Spain in the train of Cardinal Granvilla. During a prolonged stay at the Spanish Court he enriched his Flemish method by study of the portraits by Titian which the emperor had accumulated. Moro's teaching and influence started the Castile School of portrait painting. His best pupil was Alonso Sánchez Coello, (?-1590) whose portraits are vital records of personality, although somewhat trivialized by the elaboration of meticulous detail.

CHAPTER IV

A PANORAMIC VIEW

Part II: Seventeenth Century to the Present Day.

THE seventeenth century was the golden age of Spanish art, as it was of the art of Holland; product in the one case of national decline, in the other of national growth. While Spain was neglecting her national resources, losing her morale and wasting money and men on a vain effort to enslave the Dutch, the latter, in their fight for liberty, built up their national character and developed the resources of their country. Yet, under conditions so different, the genius of each people was liberated, threw off the shackles of foreign influence and discovered its own racial expression in painting. Each of the great schools had its protagonist: Valencia, José Ribera (1588-1656); Andalusia, Murillo (1618-1682); Castile, Velasquez, (1599-1660). Meanwhile, as we have noted, the early part of the century was occupied by the great artist, El Greco.

As these will be discussed in separate chapters, it remains to note the most important of the lesser painters of the period under their respective schools.

In the School of Castile the vogue of portraiture at Court was perpetuated by Coello's pupil, Juan Pantoja de la Cruz (1551-1610) and by Bartolomé Gonzáles (1564-1627). The former's portraits are hard and dry in treatment and shallow in expression, while the latter's, despite a tightness and triviality of detail, have a certain grandiose dignity of design. Witness the equestrian portraits of Philip III and his wife, Doña Margarita of Austria and that of Philip IV's first wife, Doña Isabel de Borbón. In the Prado catalogue these are still assigned to Velasquez, but latest criticism confines the latter's share in them to retouching of certain parts, particularly the horses, while giving the originals to Gonzáles. It is further believed that the landscapes in the Philip III and Queen Margarita were worked over by Velasquez's pupil and son-in-law, Mazo. The handling of the figures is so different from that of the rest of the compositions, so evidently the reverse of Velasquez's broad and pregnant style, that it is strange the canvases should ever have been assigned in their entirety to him; except for the reason that until recently it has been the custom, both in Madrid and elsewhere, to attribute to this master anything, however mediocre, which approached the appearance of his method.

We recall among the Italian painters invited to the Court of Philip II, Bartolomeo Carducho and Patricio Caxés. Each had a son who became a painter; Vicente Carducho (1585-1638) born in Italy, but educated and naturalised in Spain, and Eugenio Caxés (1577-1642), whose birthplace was Madrid. They were employed in decorating the palaces of the Prado and the Escoriál. Their work is mannered, with much technical proficiency and little inspiration. It is, however, handsome in design; wherein lies its chief interest to the student of Spanish painting, since it helped to foster that skill in the filling of a space which was brought to such perfection by Velasquez. In this connection we may mention Fray Juan Bautista Mayno (1594-1690), a Dominican monk, who had been drawing master to Philip IV before his accession and was retained by him afterwards as an adviser in matters of art. There is an "allegory" by him in the entrance hall of the Prado, representing *The Pacification of the States of Flanders* which in qualities of painting is quite uninteresting, yet, regarded as a decoration, has considerable merit, reminding one of Puvis de Chavannes' flat patterns of full and empty spaces. Indeed, one may be disposed to feel that from the point of view of mural decoration it is even superior to Velasquez's *Surrender of Breda*, which by comparison is a historical picture. It is interesting to note that Mayno was a native of Toledo and in consequence familiar with the work of El Greco, who, we shall find, was a master of decorative space-filling.

In 1603, during the reign of Philip III, Rubens, on a mission from the Duke of Mantua, visited the Spanish Court. One of the Duke's intentions was that his emissary should copy some of the masterpieces of the Royal collection. Rubens' copy of Titian's *Temptation of Adam and Eve* now hangs in the Prado, not far from the original, and it is interesting to note how the young Flemish artist has corrected and improved the composition of the old Venetian. The orders given to Rubens included a provision that he should forward his work by employing the assistance of some of the Spanish painters. He writes, saying that he will adhere to these instructions, but, he adds, "I do not approve of it, considering the short time we have at our disposal, and the incredible inadequacy and idleness of these painters and their manners, (from which may God preserve me from any resemblance!) so absolutely different to mine."

Such was Rubens impression of art in Madrid, preceding the appearance of Velasquez. In 1628 at the zenith of his fame, he paid another diplomatic visit. Philip IV was now king and appointed his favorite, Velasquez, escort to the Flemish artist. Of the latter's impression of the younger man unfortunately no records exist.

. . . .

Velasquez maintained no regular studio for pupils, yet he naturally exercised an influence on many of the younger painters of the day, and actually gave instruction to some. Among the latter the best known are Juan Bautista Martinez del Mazo and Juan Carreño, who will be considered later, and Juan de Pareja. The last mentioned was a mulatto, born in Seville about 1608, who came to Madrid with Velasquez in the capacity of a servant and remained with him all his life. Being constantly employed in the studio, he was himself inspired to become an artist; but as no slave might practise the free art of painting he worked in secret, copying his master's works. At last by a stratagem he revealed his talent. Having painted a picture with special care, he placed it in his master's studio with its face to the wall. The king, on his next visit, ordered the picture to be turned and enquired who had painted it. Whereupon Pareja went down on his knees, and implored the royal protection. The king, turning to Velasquez, said—"you will have no say in this matter and I warn you that he who possesses so much talent cannot remain a slave." At least such is the story, though it is considered more probable that Velasquez, whose generosity was marked, actually connived at the slave's education and procured his enfranchisement. But, although a free man, he continued to serve his beloved master, and after the latter's death in 1660 continued in the service of his son-in-law, Mazo, until his own death in 1670. He is represented in the Prado by the *Vocation of S. Matthew*. Christ, arrayed in the conventional draperies, is standing beside a table at which is seated Matthew, in Oriental clothes, surrounded by others in Spanish costume of the period. It is an ambitious and rather tedious picture.

Three painters of this period which call for brief notice are Antonio Pereda, Francisco Collantes and José Leonardo. Pereda (1599-1669) was born in Valladolid, but moved to Madrid to study art and remained there. In the Academy of San Fernando is an "allegory" by him, entitled *The Dream of Life*. It represents a young man of heavy, rather Dutch aspect, handsomely dressed, seated asleep before a table. The latter is strewn with a variety of objects—jewels, flowers, coins, weapons, music, a mask, a book—which contribute to the joy and fulness of life. Meanwhile, on the book rests a skull, while an angel in the background, gazing at the youth, holds a scroll inscribed—"Æterne pungit, cito volat et occidet." The picture is blackened and murky, but the still-life is rendered with remarkable naturalness. Indeed, naturalistic veracity and a taste for ascetic or moral suggestion characterises Pereda's art. Note, for example, the *S. Jerome* of the Prado where the aged saint, stripped to the waist, sits in a spiritual daze, grasping a cross of rudely joined sticks, which lies upon a book. The latter contains an engraved illustration, represented with extraordinary *vraisemblance*, and the same quality is carried to a disgusting pitch in the rendering of the withered, flabby flesh. Even more revolting and commonplace in its excessive naturalism is an adjoining *Ecce Homo*—blood that looks like blood, a rope unmistakably a rope, and a cross made out of a tree, the bark of which is realised with ridiculously ineffectual exactness. The two pictures have neither the vigor of handling nor the dignity of conception to be found in Ribera's corresponding subjects. They represent naturalism for the sake of naturalism; and anticipate the general decadence which settled down on the School of Castile toward the end of the seventeenth century.

Collantes (1599-1656), a pupil of Vincente Carducho, is represented in the Prado by a *Vision of Ezekiel*. In the foreground is confusion of opened tombs and risen bodies and skeletons; in the background the ruins of a stately classic city, and in the center, raised on an eminence, the prophet preaching to the awakened dead. The scene both in composition and chiaroscuro is quite impressive. Collantes is also represented in the Louvre by *The Burning Bush*.

José Leonardo (1616-1656) is of chief interest to the student because of his large canvas in the Prado, in which he has represented the same subject that was immortalised by Velasquez—*The Surrender of Breda*. Leonardo's composition is divided diagonally, the left foreground being occupied by the principal group, while the upper right triangle includes the background: a plain in which troops are deploying, and a distant view of the city. It is noticeable that the younger man, whose short life, clouded by mental trouble, scarcely permitted him to reach his own maturity, has, like Velasquez, made a decorative use of the lances. His conception, also, of the scene is one that probably commended itself to Spanish feeling, for he has represented the conquered Justin of Nassau submissively kneeling, as he presents the keys to his conqueror, who is on horseback. Another example by Leonardo in the Prado is the *Taking of Acqui*. It is, with the group reversed, similarly composed to the previous picture, of which it is a companion piece, both having been painted for the "Hall of the Kings" in the Palace of Buen Retiro. Notable, again, is the device of lances, while the mounted figure of the Duke de Feria, as he leads the attack, bears an unmistakable general resemblance to the equestrian portrait of the Count Olivarez by Velasquez.

Among the Italian painters summoned to Madrid by Philip II, had been a native of Bologna, Antonio Rizi. He had two sons, Juan and Francisco. Fray Juan Rizi, for he entered the Benedictine order and spent the latter part of his life in a monastery at Rome, was the pupil of Fray Juan Bautista Mayno. His portraits, bearing some resemblance to those of Velasquez, have been at times attributed to Mazo. Such was the case with the *Portrait of Don Tiburcio de Redin* in the Prado, which represents a man with curls falling to his shoulders, dressed in a handsome cavalier costume, standing beside a table. He rests one hand on it and with the other holds a large felt hat. It is a straightforward presentation of a virile personality, but painted with little verve. Far more interesting is a *Saint Benedict Celebrating Mass*, in the Academy of San Fernando. With the sacred wafer in his hand, the saint bends his strong head, with its black hair and beard, over the white altar-cloth. Over his alb is a gold embroidered white chasuble, supported by a monk in black. These figures are seen against a grey-drab wall, meanwhile a third figure, an acolyte, is in white. It is thus a very handsome tonality of grey, white and black, which gives an air of grandiose distinction to the very naturalistic way in which the whole is painted. The brother, Francisco Rizi, was a pupil of Carducho, and enjoyed reputation as a painter in fresco, decorating among other sacred edifices the Cathedral of Toledo. He was also employed as a director of scenery and stage effects in the dramatic performances given in the Palace of Buen Retiro. Apropos of these experiences, he executed a curious picture, now in the Prado, in which he has represented in an ensemble the successive stages of an auto-de-fé. It commemorates one that actually took place in the Plaza Mayor of Madrid on June 30, 1680, lasting from eight in the morning until half-past nine at night. The function had afforded a spasm of zest to the wretched religious maniac, Charles II, who commanded the painting. It contains some three thousand figures, and, considering that Rizi was seventy-five years old when he executed it, is an achievement as surprising as unnecessary.

One of Francisco Rizi's pupils was José Antolinez (1639-1676), a native of Seville. Something of southern sweetness of sentiment pervades his pictures as may be seen in *The Assumption* of the Munich Pinakothek, *The Glorification of the Virgin* in the Ryks Museum, Amsterdam and the *Ecstasy of the Magdalen*, of the Prado. The last named represents the penitent floating in a seated posture, upborne by angels. Two others hold above her the jar of ointment, while an older angel plays the lute. The drapery is of ashy purple silk brocaded with mauve arabesques, a fine passage of color suggestive of the influence of Van Dyke, which at this period began to find its way into Spain. One may discover it again in the elegantly sentimental style of Mateo Cerezo, who was originally a pupil of Carreño. Examples that may be quoted are the *Penitent Magdalen* in the Gallery of the Hague, and the *S. John the Baptist* of the Cassel Gallery, both of them characterised by affectation. A more important example, because of its decorative composition, is the *Assumption of the Virgin* in the Prado. Down below, the faithful are peering into a sarcophagus, filled

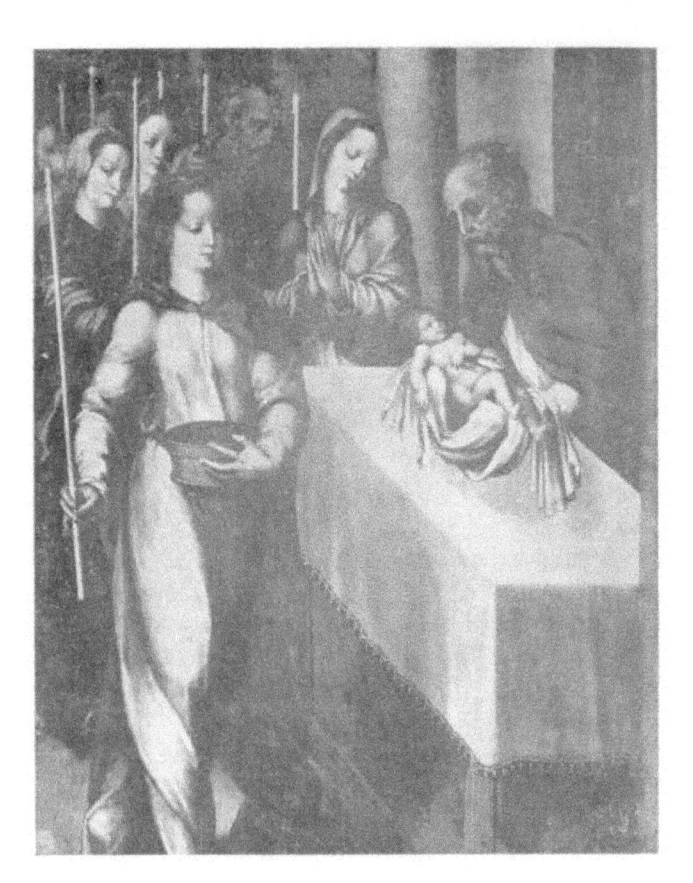

PRESENTATION OF JESUS INLUIS MORALES
  THE TEMPLE

THE PRADO

with flowers, while overhead the Virgin and her supporting angels make an elegant mass of white and blue silk and fluttering wings. But the picture is fatally pretty, characteristic of the decline of devotional feeling and artistic taste.

    This allusion to the decadence of the School of Castile which marks the end of the seventeenth century may be closed by a reference to Claudio Coello (d. 1693). The work which brought him greatest fame in his own day is the altar-piece of *La Santa Forma* at the south end of the sacristry of the Escoriál. It represents a perspective view of the room in which you are standing as you look at the picture. Thus the great school of Spanish naturalism passes out in the meretricious glamour of a looking-glass picture.

SCHOOL OF VALENCIA, SEVENTEENTH CENTURY

In the School of Valencia the connecting link between the period of mannerism, represented by Juan de Juanes, and the highest development of the naturalistic motive in the person of Ribera is supplied by Francisco Ribalta. He was born in Castellón de la Plana, between the years 1550 and 1560 and died in 1628. After studying with an unknown painter in Valencia, he spent three years in Italy, where he was particularly attracted by the works of Raphael, Sebastian del Piombo and the Caracci. Returning to Valencia, he executed a *Last Supper* for the high altar of the Church of Corpus Christi. The picture, which is still in the place for which it was painted, aroused so much enthusiasm that he was kept employed in providing works for the churches, monasteries and hospitals in and around Valencia. Some of these are distinguished by grandiose compositions and figures of noble character. But in other works Ribalta's coloring is attenuated and his handling thin; while on other occasions he exhibits a mingling of Italian "idealism" with Spanish naturalism. Examples of his poor color and technique are Nos. 946 and 949 in the Prado, which, moreover, are disfigured by their sentimentality. His particular talent, however, appears at its best in an adjacent canvas, *S. Francis d'Assisi*. The monk, clad in a brown habit, is lying on a pallet covered with a blanket. His parched yellow face and strong, nervous hands are raised in ecstasy toward an angel, playing a lute, who floats above him in well-disposed draperies of dull green and rose. Contrasted with the grace of this figure is the severely naturalistic way in which the monk and the accessories, such as an iron lamp and missal, are represented. It is a picture both of charm and force and is characteristic of the kind of influence that Ribalta exerted over his pupil, Ribera.

SCHOOL OF ANDALUSIA OF THE SEVENTEENTH CENTURY

The transition period in the School of Andalusia is filled by two men. These were Juan de las Roelas, who painted in a broad and yet seductive manner with soft, warm chiaroscuro, and the eccentric Francisco Herrera, who adapted these qualities to a "furioso" style. For this reason he has been credited with the chief influence in developing the naturalistic methods of the Andalusian School. But the credit is now assigned to Ribera, whose pictures, introduced into Seville, helped materially to shape the studies of a group of young artists which included Alonso Cano, Zurbarán, Murillo and Velasquez.

In the eighteenth century native painting declined to a condition that renders it negligible to the student. The names which occur are those of foreigners such as Luca Giordano, Tiepolo, and Raphael Mengs. Suddenly, however, toward the last quarter it sprang again to life in the genius of Goya. The latter died in 1826, and of the few names which break the monotony of Spanish painting during the nineteenth century it may be sufficient to mention those of Mariano Fortuny, Francisco Pradilla, Joaquin Sorolla y Bastida and Ignacio Zuloaga. These are to be considered later.

CHAPTER V

DOMENCO THEOTOCOPULI (EL GRECO)

DOMENCO THEOTOCOPULI was born in Crete; hence the nickname by which he was known: El Greco. He arrived in Spain by way of Venice and Rome; therefore in the catalogue of the Prado he is included among the Italian artists. It was either an excess of modesty on the part of the Spanish or a curious symptom of indifference thus to rob their own school of so great an artist. Nor has it the warrant of facts. Though El Greco had been a pupil of Titian and had drawn inspiration from Tintoretto, it is the fact of his art being so different from that of Italy, of his developing so unique a personality of his own, that is the distinguishing feature of his genius. Moreover, it was not until after his arrival in Spain and a sojourn of some time in Toledo that he discovered himself. It was the conditions, physical and spiritual, of his adopted country that brought to maturity the real El Greco. Spain drew forth his genius and in return he expressed the genius of the Spanish race in its spiritual aspects to a higher degree than any other artist of Spain. He was the seer, the diviner, who not only mirrored the external character of his times but also realised its soul.

The Church of his day seems to have prized his genius: the king underrated it, while contemporaries and posterity recognising him as bizarre, inclined to the theory that he was mad. It has been left to the judgment of the present day, reaching back scarcely more than twenty years, to appraise El Greco at his real valuation. The reasons for both the earlier and the most recent estimations are plain.

Philip II, patron of Titian, was enamoured of Italian art and, as we recall, imported Italian artists to decorate his palaces. Being a man of small and dogmatic mind he could not extend appreciation to work so different as El Greco's, and set the fashion among laymen to ignore it. Later the whole trend of Spanish art in its emergence from Italianate imitation was toward naturalism. The seventeenth century was overshadowed by the genius of Velasquez. In the eighteenth century Spain followed the lead of other countries in the academic effort to revive the forms without the spirit of the Renaissance art, until she became suddenly aware of a native genius: Goya, the temperamental, objective, impressionist. The nineteenth century was occupied with the rediscovery of Velasquez. Its watchword became "truth"; truth of actual appearances, the seeing and rendering of objective facts as they really seem to be. Its artistic motive, in fact, notwithstanding that it included, as it could not help doing, the limitations and variations of the personal equation, was in essence photographic. It was concerned, like the camera, with what the eye can see. Not until the end of the century did this vogue of objective naturalism abate. The inevitable reaction against this naturalistic view of art set in; quickened by the gradual realisation that photography was crowding the painter from their common field of sight. Artists, on the one hand, began to realise that there are internal as well as external facts, facts of the spirit as well as facts of matter; and, on the other, that the chief value of a picture is not in its making something look like life, but in extracting from the life represented its fullest amount of expression. Expression, among progressive modern artists, has taken precedence of mere representation. It is therefore, our own day that is giving special honor to El Greco and Goya; to Goya, the master of material expression, to El Greco who joined this, in so extraordinary a degree, to spiritual expression.

Having thus established the point of view from which El Greco should be studied, we will briefly consider the conditions under which his genius developed and then the qualities, technical and spiritual, which his works exhibit. We shall find that he broke away from the Venetian use of color, employing a sober range of hues, of extreme subtlety and a chiaroscuro all his own. That he was also a great master of composition, decorating every part of his large canvases with meaningful details, so that there are no spaces perfunctorily filled or devoid of interest. A great draughtsman also, who, although he altered for his own purpose the proportions of figures and at times dared to indulge in "bad drawing," realises the plastic qualities of form as few artists have done, and extracts from form, gesture and action a maximum of character and expression. Similarly, in his portraits we shall discover not only a vivid rendering of external personality, but also a penetrating insight into the soul of the subject. Finally, in the presence of his work one should be conscious of a rare and elevated spirit, the artist's own, interpreting the spiritual genius of the Spain of his day.

. . . .

Almost nothing is known of El Greco's life. No record of him exists until November 16, 1570, the date of a letter written by the Venetian miniature painter, Julio Clovio to Cardinal Nepote Farnese. It says—"There is in Rome a young man from Candia, a disciple of Titian, who in my opinion is a painter of rare talent. Among other things he has painted a portrait of himself, which causes wonderment to all the painters of Rome. I should like him to be under the patronage of your Illustrious and Reverend Lordship, without any other contribution toward his livelihood than a room in the Farnese Palace for some little time, until he can find other accommodation." This letter establishes El Greco's birthplace, corroborating the artist's signature, as it appears on many canvases in Greek characters with the addition of "Cretan"; his experience under Titian in Venice; his visit to Rome and the fact that in the year 1570 he was a young man. How long he stayed in Rome is uncertain, but the next date of certainty, 1577, appears after his signature upon a picture of *The Assumption of the Virgin* for the Church of San Domingo el Antigua in Toledo. The fact of El Greco being engaged on this work is corroborated by documents relating to the church, in which it is recorded that the artist was paid 1000 ducats for eight pictures to adorn the high and side altars. Thus it appears that at some date between the years 1570 and 1577 El Greco reached Spain and settled in Toledo. Here he seems to have lived continuously until his death, the record of which is still preserved. "On 7th April, 1614, died Domenico Greco. He left no will. He received the sacraments, was buried in Santo Domingo el Antigua; and gave candles." The position of El Greco's tomb in San Domingo is not known. The only other documents in existence relate to contracts for commissions and occasional disputes and lawsuits over the prices. They have been summarised and used as data for establishing the order in which his pictures were executed by Albert F. Calvert and E. Gasquoine Hartley in their critical and richly illustrated book, "El Greco, An Account of his Life and Works."

One document may be mentioned here, since it indicates El Greco's brief relations with the Court. It is a royal order, dated 1580, which states that a commission had been entrusted to Domenico Theotocopuli, Greek painter, residing in Toledo, but that "the work was not being carried on for want of money and fine colors." Therefore it is commanded, "That the said painter be supplied with money, also with the fine colors that he asks for, and, especially ultramarine, that the work may be executed with brevity as is suitable in my service."

Since El Greco had finished his commission for Santo Domingo and had also painted an altar piece, *El Expolio*, or *Christ Despoiled of His Raiment on Calvary*, for the Cathedral, it would seem as if his plea of no

THE CRUCIFIXION   EL GRECO

THE LOUVRE

money and colors had been a pretence for avoiding, if possible, the execution of the Royal commission. The outcome of the affair is described by a Father Siguenza, writing in 1605. "There is here in the Salas Capitulares of the Escoriál, a picture of *San Maurico and His Soldiers* by a Domenico Greco, who has come to Toledo and there made excellent things. The picture was designed for the proper altar of the Saint, but it did not satisfy His Majesty. It is not much, because it satisfies few; though they say that it has great art, and that its author has much knowledge and that excellent things can be seen from his hand."

El Greco had one son, George Manuel, who was appointed architect of the Cathedral. He also practised sculpture and painting, in the latter medium imitating his father's style so closely that some of the son's pictures have been attributed to him. The portrait of a beautiful girl, late the property of Sir John Stirling-Maxwell and now in the National Gallery,

London, has been called the artist's daughter; but later criticism assigns this painting either to Tintoretto or to El Greco's early Italian period when he was still a young man. The portrait of his son George, is identified in the *San Martin* of San José, and again as the youth who holds the map in the *Vista of Toledo*. It is also supposed to exist in the younger figure of the boy on the left of the composition of *The Funeral of Count Orgaz*. In the latter it has also been suggested that the face with the pointed beard, sixth from the right, represents El Greco himself; while tradition also attributes the title of *Self Portrait of the Artist* to the picture in the Seville Museum of a man of middle age, holding a brush and palette. These, however, are only surmises.

The mystery that surrounds the life of El Greco is perhaps a little lifted by the account of him which Guiseppe Martinez gives in his "Practical Letters on the Art of Painting." It is not the evidence of a contemporary, but of one who probably got his impressions from those who had known the artist or at least the opinion commonly held of him during his life.

"At that time there came from Italy a painter called Dominico Greco; it is said that he was a pupil of Titian. He settled in the famous and ancient city of Toledo, introducing such an extravagant style that to this day nothing has been seen to equal it; attempting to discuss it would cause confusion in the soundest minds; his works being so dissimilar that they do not seem to be by the same hand. He came to this city with a high reputation, so much so that he gave it to be understood that there was nothing superior to his works. In truth he achieved some works which are worthy of estimation and which can be put among those of famous painters. His nature was extravagant like his painting. It is not known with certainty what he did with his works, as he used to say no price was high enough for them, and so he gave them in pledge to their owners who willingly advanced him what he asked for. He earned many ducats, but spent them in too great pomp and display in his house, to the extent of keeping paid musicians to entertain him at meal times. His works were many, but the only wealth he left were two hundred unfinished paintings; he reached an advanced age, always enjoying great fame. He was a famous architect and very eloquent in his speeches. He had few disciples, as none cared to follow his capricious and extravagant style, which was only suitable for himself."

We get a glimpse here of a strangely individual personality, reserved and proud, conscious of his destiny, working it out in a haughty exclusiveness; wrapt up in high thoughts and cultivating in the retirement of private life a rare refinement. In Toledo, then the citadel of the Catholic Faith, so dominated by the dignitaries of the Church that Philip II, who brooked no rivalry of power, was forced to transfer his Court thence to

Madrid, El Greco preserved the integrity of his artistic faith and, by separating himself from outside influences, maintained the independent sovereignty of his own ideals.

. . . .

El Greco left a *View of Toledo*; a portrait, one would rather call it, of a city's appearance and her soul; a highly interpretative vision of the impression of Toledo's soul upon the spiritual imagination of the artist. The view is from the hill beneath which the present railroad station lies, and looks across the broken ground to the ravine of the Tagus. In the middle distance toward the left it is spanned by the wide arch and its narrower sister of the Alcántara bridge. Thence the line of the city walls, interrupted by their Moorish towers, mount the citadel hill to the group of buildings that crown the summit. The Alcázar and the north tower of the cathedral stand conspicuously against a sky, tumultuous with emotion and lit with large aspiring clouds. These, like the architecture, catch the sharpest light, which elsewhere is distributed in masses of lower tone; a union of quiet illumination and of flashing sword-like brands of light, characteristic of so many of the artist's compositions, so suggestive of passionate inspiration.

How different from Venice of his youth, this rock-rooted fortress city of the artist's adoption! No less proudly aloof, but sternly and strenuously exalted; straitened within tortuous limits; an apex once of Moorish power and luxury, now of Catholic dominion and sumptuous ecclesiastical ceremony; its dignitaries men of high and commanding personality, its Cathedral famous throughout Spain as Toledo the Rich! The chivalric fervor bred upon countless battlefields, glowed here in an intense heat of religious mysticism. Her hidalgos, "sons of somebody," were among the proudest of their class, self-contained, austere, yet fired with religious ecstasy. Toledo was at that time the soul of Catholicism and of the high-bred Chivalry of Castile.

El Greco, with the penetration of the alien observer, caught its spirit. It inflamed his own romantic ardor and religious devoutness; at the same time giving fibre and force to his imagination. Yet his whole art, as it developed under these conditions, was built up on observed facts. The type of his figures, both in portraiture and altar-pieces, was drawn from the humanity about him, the lean, long-limbed bodies, with high narrow heads; a type that still survives. You see it even in Madrid, still more readily in Toledo. Here too in the passing throng you may detect one of those wistful,

SAN MAURICIO AND HIS THEBAN LEGION — EL GRECO

THE ESCORIÁL

flower-like faces, pure as the chalice of a lily, that El Greco learned to give to his Madonnas, while among the children you will find the strangely sexless, coldly passionate faces of his angels.

    He exaggerated the type, just as his contemporary, Cervantes did; the latter to make it ridiculous, El Greco in sympathy with its high enthusiasm. But each from his own standpoint captured the real soul of the Spanish race more effectively than any other writer or artist of Spain. The humor of Cervantes made him intensely popular, the seriousness of El Greco has had to wait until to-day for recognition. His exaggeration, sometimes even approaching distortion, is for the purpose of decorative effect or for enforcing character or emotion, or is more frequently employed with the two purposes combined.

A fine example of characterization is the portrait, here called *S. Jerome* (Frontispiece). There are replicas of this picture in the National Gallery and the Prado, where it is called *S. Paul*. But the title is of small account. The picture is clearly the portrait of some dignitary of the Church or at least of the type of ecclesiastics of the day. The stubby hair and the long beard are approaching white, the face is greyed over, and silvery lights relieve the rose colored mantle. The head, in proportion to the body is small but of extra length and narrowness, and the hands are extremely elongated. But by these exaggerations what expression of character is obtained! The head is at once that of a soldier, a scholar and an ascetic. The eyes have a cold, piercing directness; the long nose is indicative of relentless purpose and the mouth of iron rigidity and cruelty. One hand lies on the book with a gesture of refinement, almost of tenderness, while the thumb of the other is turned down with a decision that brooks no reasoning or opposition. In fine, the type is a strange mixture of intellectuality and bigotry; of elevation and narrowness, of gentleness and remorselessness. It might be that of an inquisitor, who condemns with no more hesitation than a surgeon, compelled by his diagnosis to use the knife.

Or for an example of distortion, employed with emotional effect, turn to *The Crucifixion* of the Louvre (p. 70). The body of the Christ is beautiful in its languor of repose; no pain or horror mars the serenity. The tragedy of the event is depicted in the amazing impression of the sky; a murky blackish green veil, rent like the veil of the Temple, with scars of white. The Saviour rests from his labors. It is the universal tragedy of sin which will crucify him afresh, that is depicted. For my own part, I know of no other suggestion of the Divine Tragedy so spiritually moving as this one. El Greco painted this subject several times. Another fine example is *The Crucifixion* of the Prado, where the figures of the donor and an ecclesiastic are replaced by the three Maries and S. John, figures expressive of anguish and adoration, while angels of spiritual loveliness receive in their hands with transports of adoring ecstasy the blood from the sacred wounds. It is at once a pæan and a dirge, superb in its decorative elaboration. But in the picture of the Louvre, the decorative scheme is sublimely elemental; its very simplicity

THE FUNERAL OF COUNT　　　　　　　　EL GRECO
　　　　ORGAZ

SAN TOMÉ, TOLEDO

augments the poignancy of the appeal. But our original consideration was the distortion introduced. The natural appearance of the sky is distorted; the color false, there is no suggestion of actual light or atmosphere. There was, in fact, no thought of representing the sky naturally; it has been used as a symbol of expression. And it was so that El Greco chose at times to use form.

If the student peers through the spectacles of an academic pedagogue, criticising this or that because it does not conform to his canons of proportion or notions of correct drawing, he will never discover the real El Greco. If he is looking solely or chiefly for naturalistic representation, such as will pass muster in the schools, let him turn away at once. Otherwise he will be only seeking for trouble. It is with the eye of the imagination, seeking for spiritual impressions or for character of expression and expression of character, that El Greco must be studied. On the other hand, it must not be supposed that El Greco was indifferent to the facts of form. No artist better understood and valued form or rendered it with more reliance on its plastic qualities. It was, however, not the plasticity merely of its shape that attracted him, but its plasticity of expression. He made expression visible in its external appearances. He used form as an instrument of interpretation; hence, for the furtherance of expression he dared to exaggerate or even to distort it.

It is not amiss to compare El Greco to some great composer whose medium is his orchestra. The latter is made up of units, but there is no established proportion of the relation which they bear to each other and to the whole. It is a flexible instrument in which the composer makes his own adjustments. If for the interpretation of his theme he exaggerates the wind instruments or chooses to introduce new devices for attaining an effect, he is judged solely by the harmonious result. For music being a completely abstract art, the verdict depends upon the structure, scope and quality of its expression. The art of painting is less abstract, being limited by the sense appreciation of the eye and the need of attaching the expression to some visible object; but, as far as possible with the liberty of the musical composer, El Greco composed his symphonies of form and color.

. . . .

This liberty of composition was only gradually evolved. His earlier work, executed during his first years in Toledo, exhibit traces of his Venetian training. *The Assumption of the Virgin*, which is now owned by the Art Institute of Chicago, is in its treatment of the forms and composition still Titianesque; but already the influence of the new environment upon El Greco's individuality is apparent. He has caught as yet little if any of the mystic fervor, but the types, particularly of the apostles, are local; the draperies are handled broadly and plastically, and the color is no longer of Venetian sumptuousness. The process of dematerialization has begun, which will be carried on until in the great works of the artist's maturity the Venetian richness of pigment, full of mundane splendor, has entirely disappeared in cool, austere harmonies of blue, lemon and yellow, black, grey, white, olive green and silvery carnation. Touches of warm color occur but they are comparatively rare. Least of all in the great altarpiece does El Greco use color for effects of pageantry or mere decoration. His use is interpretative of spiritual significance. In his portraits it is psychologically expressive.

The latter are mostly half-lengths or busts; grand, pale faces against a sombre background, isolated by a white ruff from the black body on which the white nervous hands are displayed. On the other hand, the portraits of ecclesiastics or imaginary presentation of saints involve a variety of hues. There is a series of such presentments of the apostles in the little Provincial Museum, now established in El Greco's house. The *S. Bartholomew* is entirely in white, but the others are bi-colored, showing a robe and mantle, respectively of yellow and blue, yellow-green and red-wine color, grey-blue and orange, grey-blue and apple green, and so on. It is as though the artist had searched for the most unusual and *recherché* combinations and had compelled them into harmony by the nuances with which he has invested them. Moreover, each is in psychological relation to the head and hands of the subject. Another point to be observed in El Greco's use of color is that he did not spread his pigment thin over an underpainting of light and dark, but actually modeled in color, obtaining the chiaroscuro by means of values.

It is with a feeling of strangeness that one views a number of El Greco's portraits such as is gathered in the Prado. Almost invariably the eyes are fixed on us, but with no look of recognition or sympathy. Though the face thrills with life, it is impassive. Behind each living mask is an impenetrable mind, wrapped completely in the seclusion of its own spirit. Equally removed from all outside sympathies are the faces of the apostles and saints. They, however, are not impassive, for on each is the trace of inward struggle, of highly wrought meditation or spiritual ecstasy. Their personalities are so varied and distinct that one is assured they are portraits or at least studies of the types of ecclesiastics, monks or laymen which Toledo presented. They have one quality in common, that of transcendental elevation; symptomatic of the spiritual unrest of the time. For elsewhere the Protestant Reformation was making headway and Spain was its most ardent opponent. It was here that the Counter-Reformation reached its most extravagant form. The Spaniard met the challenge of reason with a passionate belief, which developed into mysticism and visionary exaltation. Of this Toledo was the volcanic center and El Greco its pictorial exponent. The mainspring of his motive was his own intense religious belief, which enabled him to give plastic reality to the visions of his passionately exalted imagination.

. . . .

His pictures, when he has adjusted his style to his motive, are all visions. Even his portraits are visions of men's souls. And the secret of his power to suggest the reality of the vision is that it is based on realism. His creations are a union of realism and idealism; or rather of realism in the true sense. For to-day we have learnt to distinguish between realism and naturalism:

BAPTISM OF CHRIST   EL GRECO

THE PRADO

the latter a representation of natural phenomena; realism a representation of the same with a suggestion of their relation to the horizon of the idea involved in them. This becomes El Greco's almost invariable habit. Turn, for example, to the *San Mauricio* (p. 75), which was executed shortly after the *Assumption of the Virgin*. According to legend Mauritius was the general of a Theban mercenary legion in the Roman army. He refused to pay homage to the gods and was condemned to be beheaded. Whereupon the whole legion declared their faith and shared martyrdom with their leader. One may believe that El Greco pictured the event in his imagination; its several phases, the general's refusal, the executions and the glory in Heaven of the martyr's crown. In the glow of religious fervor a vision shaped itself before the eyes of his spirit and he set it upon the canvas. The noble heads of the general and his lieutenants are clearly portraits of contemporaries, of men who no doubt believed themselves capable of imitating the example of the saint, if occasion required it. At the outset, therefore, the picture is based, not on a mere representation of certain persons, but of the latter in their relation to the idea involved. In the gravity and confidence of the saint's face are mirrored alike the consciousness of the tragedy to be depicted and the glory that will follow. The saint himself, in fact, is represented as having his own vision of the situation in relation to its horizon of ideas.

The back of the officer who is delivering the ultimatum is modeled with intentional exaggeration, to increase the refined suggestion of the saint and at the same time to emphasise the separateness of the main group both from the scene that is being enacted in the rear and from the Heavenly vision. The color impression of the whole picture is blue; cold tones of blue relieved by the pale red-wine color of the flag, the pale creamy yellow of some of the corselets and the extreme white of the flesh. It is a scheme which gives an extraordinary suggestion of abstraction. The lighting also reveals the beginning of El Greco's gradually developed method of chiaroscuro. The latter grew out of his study to give to every part of the decorative pattern of his composition the life of movement. In the figures of the angels actual movement is expressed in the gestures and actions, but in the stationary figures in the foreground it is suggested by the curling, quivering light, especially on the legs. These light effects, so characteristic of El Greco's work from this point onward, will embarrass the student who is looking for naturalistic exactitude. It is not until he has become used to the artist's blending of the concrete and the abstract, that he will realise its fitness in the whole scheme of the vision.

The next great work of El Greco's career was *The Funeral of Count Orgaz*, (p. 76), known in Spain as *El Interrio*. This masterpiece still hangs in the church for which it was painted, San Tomé, in Toledo. It commemorates the legend connected with the founder of the church, the pious Count Orgaz, who died in 1323. At his funeral S.S. Augustine and Stephen appeared and lowered the body into the grave. Once more it is a vision both of the actualities of the incident and of the no less reality of the spiritual idea involved. While the priests and faithful friends, portrait-studies of El Greco's contemporaries, assist at the solemn function, some turn their eyes to the vision above, where amid the hosts of prophets, apostles, saints and angels, with the Blessed Virgin interceding, the naked soul of the Count appears at the feet of his Redeemer. Was ever nakedness expressed so literally and yet with such abstraction? The whole vision is illuminated by a cold light which comes from within the scene itself. The sumptuousness of gold embroidery distinguishes the vestments of the two saints in the foreground, emblematic of the opulent ceremonial of the Catholic Church, while the Chivalry of Spain is commemorated in the dead body. The black steel of the armor against the ivory white of the sheet sets the key of black and white which is the general color impression of the lower part of the picture. Above, the Virgin's mantle makes a positive note of blue among the paler and higher tones of the same color, the pale yellow, cream and occasional suggestion of mauve and faintest carmine.

The prominence given to the Virgin and the nude form, and the elongation of the latter help to isolate the Christ and increase the sense of altitude, up toward which are straining eagerly the faces of the Heavenly hosts. What a pageant of spiritual exaltation, parted by open tableau-curtains of cloud from the drama below! And the latter—was ever a greater intensity of gravity, dignity and tenderness compressed into a group of heads? Tradition has it that the priest to the right in white vestment is Don Andrez Nuñez, priest of San Tomé. The grey-bearded profile to his left is known to be a portrait of the painter, Antonio Corrubias, whose brother, Diego, appears in the white-bearded man on the left of the composition, above the figure of S. Stephen. The face with the ruff, to the left of Antonio Corrubias, is supposed to be the artist's.

Everyone has praised the consummate characterisation and technical mastery of this lower part of the picture; but many have criticised the upper and been unable to accept it as a reasonable part of the composition. On the other hand, if study of the picture include communion with the spirit and purpose which inspired it, one is brought to feel that upper and lower parts are indivisibly associated both in the conception of the subject and in the rendering of it. The composition for a moment recalls Raphael's vision of the *Disputá*, which El Greco must have seen in the Stanza of the Vatican. There, the space to be filled, though proportionately broader than this one is similarly arched, and a band of figures, representing the Church on Earth, spreads across the lower part, while in the upper, Heaven is unfolded. But beyond this all resemblance ceases. Even the earthly group in Raphael's fresco is disposed in the manner of Italian idealism; in the *Count Orgaz* its naturalness is characteristically Spanish. In the upper part of his painting Raphael continued the geometrical design of the composition by arranging the Heavenly hosts in arcs. El Greco has invented a sort of irregular, spontaneous geometry. The design has a central group of three figures, disposed to form a triangle, outside of which the spaces of cloud are divided

VIRGIN AND SAINTS   EL GRECO

SAN JOSÉ, TOLEDO

into compartments or pockets, filled with figures. It is a borrowed motive, discoverable in the compositions of Giotto and other primitive Italians and in the mosaics that helped to inspire them. It is, in fact, Byzantine. But the latter term is merely a named and dated milestone on the road which stretches back in endless perspective through Persia to Buddhistic art. Today, with our opportunities of studying the latter, we can detect a curious affinity between El Greco's arrangement and well known features of Chinese composition. Unconsciously, in fact, his genius leaped back of its conscious source to the remote spring of Oriental inspiration.

. . . .

Following the *Count Orgaz* came a series of pictures in which passionate ecstasy reached its highest intensity. Three of them are in the Prado: *The Crucifixion*, already alluded to, in which angels are catching the sacred Blood, a *Resurrection* and *The Baptism of Christ*. The last named (p. 81) is not merely a representation of one man pouring water on the head of another, whose humble mien, coupled with the introduction of a hovering dove and sometimes a venerable aged man above, tells one that the picture is meant to represent the baptism of the Second Person of the Holy Trinity. Such is generally the jejune method of treating the subject. But here we are again in the presence of a vision, in which the real spiritual significance of the facts of the incident are made visible to the eye. Heaven joins with earth in a symphonic burst of devotional enthusiasm. Movement of life abounds, the soul's life typified by human forms. There is even the rhythm of movement in the comparatively static figures of the Christ and S. John; in the angels that lift the crimson mantle and those who stand by adoring; while over head the spiritual energy mounts in wave upon wave of jubilance till it circles about the serene figure of the Most High God. Once more we note how a sense of far-off isolation is given to this topmost figure by introduction of taller angels in the front plane; also that there is nowhere any space unfilled with meaning, even the grey-green creamy clouds seeming to mount upward with their angelic burdens. But beyond all possibility of description is the degree to which the picture kindles and lifts the imagination.

Amazing also is *The Resurrection*, now in the Prado. The figure of the Lord, long and supple as a reed, is poised above, while down below the soldiers are in agitated consternation. They have been roused out of sleep by the shock of the rending tomb and, still dazed, confront the miracle. One has fallen backward in his fear, some shield their eyes from the light, while others carve the air with their swords in frantic efforts. With the exception of one fine young figure that reaches up his hand, as if in acknowledgment of the miracle, they are all nude, the bodies wrought to extreme tension of expression.

. . . .

To this time also belongs *The Dream of Philip II*, in the Escoriál. It was followed by a period of serener pictures, such as those which were painted for the Chapel of San José, Toledo. The finest of these, and the best known, is a narrow upright panel, the *S. Martin*, dividing his cloak with a nude beggar. The youthful figure of the saint—a portrait of the artist's son George, in the beauty of his first manhood—clad in black armor, is mounted on a white horse which has black accoutrements. The animal has one foreleg lifted and arched; the others parallel the legs of the beggar, recalling somewhat the treatment of the legs in the *San Mauricio*. The two figures are seen against the sky, which soars above a distant view of Toledo. In the statuesque plasticity of the forms and the chastity of the color scheme of white, black, green and pale greyish blue the picture is one of extraordinary nobility and tenderness and of extreme abstraction. Facing it is the exquisitely tender and reverential *Virgin and Saints* (p. 85) in which perhaps, more than in any other of his works El Greco has yielded to the charm of facial loveliness. Above the high altar hangs the *Coronation of the Virgin*. The center of the composition is a trefoil arrangement of the three figures of the Father, Son and Virgin, beneath which are two adoring figures, the rest of the pattern consisting of clouds in arc-like forms only less full of expressional value than the figures. It is a motive that Velasquez borrowed in his picture in the Prado of the same subject.

To this period is attributed the *Crucifixion* in the Louvre (p. 70) to which allusion has been already made. Let us note afresh the infinite calm of the Saviour's form as characteristic of this period of spiritual calm in the artist's own genius. By this time, also, we are better able to judge the introduction of the two worshippers in the lower foreground. They were probably included of necessity, representing the donor and the priest of the Church for which this picture was painted. But they also introduce that touch of naturalism, dear to the Spanish imagination; and the artist has made them contributary to his conception of the scene as a vision. It is a vision of the holy scene which these men of his own time are contemplating and the contrast of their reality lends to the vision an increased abstraction.

Also to this period chiefly belong the many *Annunciations* and *Holy Families*. Of the latter we have a fine example in the Hispanic Museum, New York, which recalls with certain modifications that of the Prado. In all these subjects the type of Madonna is drawn from the people. But it is not left in its stolid plainness as by Velasquez in his *Adoration of the Kings*, or sentimentalised as by Murillo. By El Greco it has been rarified, purged alike of grossness and earthly emotion; in fact, spiritualized. We may also assign to this period the small *Santiago* of the Metropolitan Museum, New York; exquisitely choice in its tonal scheme of blue, slightly relieved by dull ochre yellow, yet virile in handling and inspired by an exalted purity of imagination.

. . . .

To the artist's latest period belongs another picture in the Metropolitan Museum, *The Nativity*. It is the product of a newly awakened ardor, such as characterises the most important work of El Greco's closing life. The participants in the event are lowly folk; the Mother a girl of the people; the shepherds large-modeled, shrewdly featured peasants. But all are possessed with the exaltation of the moment; their naiveté and crudity are caught up in a frenzy of amazement. In the darkness of the night the scene is all aflame with spiritual incandescence. How marvellously the light and obscurity are interwoven! What a strange diversity of plastic forms and subtlety of sober coloring are wrought into the composition! Strangeness is certainly the first impression one experiences; then, following it, a realisation of intense inspiration and of masterful creativeness. One is in the presence of the unusual, of a great imaginative spirit.

Similarly ecstatic is the vision of *The Coming of the Holy Ghost* in the Prado. At the top, the Dove in Glory; under it, a horizontal row of figures, the Virgin in the center, the heads of all tipped with flame; down below, two figures, leaning back and gazing up at the Divine Glory. Some recollection of the old Titianesque crimsons and blues appears, but nothing of their mundane qualities. The whole conception is one of passionate receptivity toward the illumination from on high. The final expression of tempestuous energy appears in the *Death of Laocoon and His Son* in San Telmo, Seville and in the *Apocalypse*, or as it has been wrongly called, *The Sacred and Profane Love*, owned by the artist, Señor Zuloaga.

El Greco had pupils but left no followers. Some of his pupils, Luis Tristan, for example, and his son, George Manuel, learned to imitate his manner sufficiently closely to have caused confusion in the attribution of certain pictures. But El Greco's style was so directly the product of his own intellectuality, sensitive and passionate æsthetic imagination and highly wrought soul, that it could not be absorbed in its integrity by others. But his art influenced no less a master than the great Velasquez. We have noted that the latter borrowed from the Toledan artist his composition for the *Coronation of the Virgin* and may add the debt which his portrait of *Innocent X* appears to owe to El Greco's *Don Fernando Nino de Guevara*. It was however in the matter of color that the influence is most marked. Velasquez adopted, as Señor de Beruete says, "certain silver-grey tints in the coloring of the flesh, the use of special carmines and a greater freedom of execution in the draperies, fabrics and other accessories." These same qualities, and the intellectuality and abstraction of his conception and style have begun to affect some modern artists. The most notable example was the late Paul Cézanne, whose work, in turn, is exerting a potent influence on others. Meanwhile El Greco's pictures, until recent years known only to a few connoisseurs, are being sought for and treasured by collectors and museums.

Meanwhile, by the young painter of to-day El Greco should be studied closely. For the modern age in every development of life is beginning to demand intellectuality, and in painting particularly a greater degree of subtlety and abstract suggestion. The quality of expression is growing more and more to be the test by which the artist of the present and the future will be judged. El Greco, in all these respects is a master to be followed; not in the way of imitation, but for the sake of the principles involved in his conception of a subject and its technical rendering, and also because he will help to an understanding of other great artists of expression, such as Michelangelo, Giotto, the nameless artists of the Byzantine period and the known and unknown masters of Buddhistic art.

CHAPTER VI

VELASQUEZ

WHILE El Greco gave expression to the soul of Spanish chivalry and religion, Velasquez embodied in its highest form the racial love of naturalism. More than this, he stands above all other naturalistic painters in truth of representation.

He is usually called a realist. But modern thought is investing this term with a meaning that differentiates it from naturalism. Its use of the word is akin to the philosophic meaning of realism, which recognises the reality not only of the species or individual but also of the genus, and considers the individual as a phase of the universal process which causes it. Modern thought, in fact, applies the word realist to one who views the particular in relation to the horizon at the back of it, to the universal process of which it is a temporary manifestation. Thus it calls Ibsen a realist, because, for example, in "A Doll's House," he treats *Nora* and her husband as phases of the universal problem of marital relations. On the contrary, the playwright who presents merely a cross-section of life, characters and incidents that are true to life but are not treated in relation to the large horizon of ideas, governing our principles of living, it calls a naturalist. The distinction is a vital one and so clarifying to thought and understanding,

PHILIP IV, OLD VELASQUEZ

THE NATIONAL GALLERY

that to have once comprehended it should be to adopt it.

In the light of this distinction is Velasquez a naturalist or a realist? In his portraits, which represent his supreme achievement, is one conscious of anything but the absorbing realisation of an individual personality? Do we think of them as typical of their time and country, as are the subjects of El Greco's portraits? Most certainly there is a great exception in the marvelous *Portrait of Pope Innocent X*. Behind his grim face extends a wide horizon of correlated ideas. The psychological revelation and universal suggestion of this portrait seem to declare that Velasquez was in mind a realist, but compelled by the circumstances of his life to be a naturalist. Tethered to the Court, he was chiefly occupied with painting the royal personages and their immediate entourage. His was a scene, closed in, like a stage-scene by the artificial routine of ceremony and punctiliousness, in which the puppets, from Philip down to his dwarf play-things, posed. How could a realist portray them in relation to the horizon of ideas involved except by making them contemptible or ridiculous? But his duty as a Court painter compelled Velasquez to close out the horizon, and to represent these individuals with as much of dignity as possible. It is a noteworthy fact that the *Innocent X* was painted during the artist's second visit to Italy; while he was for a brief space quit of the cramped conditions of his life, able to look out on men and things and study them in relation to large issues. Also, the fact of it being his second visit and that he was in the full maturity of his powers, implies much. He was less preoccupied with individual impressions, more capable and disposed to view even the Pope himself in relation to the political and spiritual conditions of Rome and of the World.

But though Velasquez was compelled to be habitually a naturalist, he not only avoided the commonplace which so frequently attaches to naturalism, but proved himself the greatest naturalist in the whole story of painting. He lifted naturalism to its highest pitch of expression. His representations of life are characterised not only by living actuality, but by consummate justness, high distinction and extraordinary beauty. There is in all a union of mental supremacy and of supreme technical artistry. Perhaps only Rembrandt, Hals and Raeburn give one so realising a sense of being in the presence of a living personality, as we experience before nearly all the portraits of Velasquez. With Rembrandt we are usually conscious of an inseeing eye which penetrates the soul of his subject and views it in relation to a wide horizon; for Rembrandt is the great realist. Velasquez, on the other hand, shares with Hals and the Scottish artist their restricted vision; but his is the finer, suggesting his own finer quality of mind. Their minds were incapable of the high seriousness, the noble aloofness of his. Hals, seen at his best in the Haarlem groups, is one of the jolly fellows he is depicting; Raeburn, an honest, sturdy gentleman among the gentry who sit to him. Velasquez is always the aristocrat, looking out upon his subject from the elevation of a superior mental dignity. It was because of this that his portraits have the supreme *cachet* of all great art: aloofness. The separateness of his own mental personality from the ordinary thing around him is communicated to the personages which he creates. They are alone with themselves; whether monarch, dwarf or beggar, separated from the common touch by virtue of their author's art. In their remoteness they are akin to Jan Van Eyck's portrait of *Jean Arnolfini and his Wife* and Holbein's *George Gyze* and *Erasmus*; but these have not the insistent suggestion of being actually alive. We recognise in them an extraordinary illusion of life; but in front of *Philip IV* in the National Gallery, of *Moenippus* and *Las Meninas* in the Prado, not to mention other examples, the consciousness of illusion does not enter our thoughts. We are face to face with truth; "verdad, no pintura," as Velasquez himself used to say was his ideal— "truth, not painting." On the other hand, the truth is saved from being merely lifelike, obvious, by the rarifying quality of Velasquez's own aloofness. His portraits quiver on the razor-edge of truth and abstraction.

We have spoken of their consummate justness. This represents another result of the high-bred nature of Velasquez's mind; revealed in a tact of selection, exposition and arrangement. He had an unerring feeling for essentials, his most characteristic works being singularly sparing of detail; a cultivated instinct for the salient gesture and expression, and a rarely economical method of achieving them. His ability to plant a figure on the floor, so that it bears down with its own weight and grows up in its own strength; to give it characteristic action, at once unified and rhythmic; to invest its contour lines with firmness and precision as well as subtlety; to give to the smallest details, such as the modeling of a glove, an individual character and, finally, to adjust all these several qualities into an organized unity and place the ensemble in perfect relation to the open space it occupies—his ability to do all this is the measure of his justness.

To the high distinction of the result we have already alluded in speaking of its dignity and aloofness. It is the product, alike, of elevated mentality and of supreme technical accomplishment. The latter brings us in touch with the cause of its extraordinary beauty.

What does beauty mean to us? If it is beauty of face and form—the easy way to artistic beauty and to lay appreciation thereof—we shall seldom find it in Velasquez's pictures. The people whom it was his lot to paint were mostly plain-featured, to use no harsher terms; their costumes outrageously extravagant and not in the direction of elegance; the coloring was sombre, only sparingly relieved with gaiety of color. Nor, for the most part, were they people of force of character or with suggestion of experience imprinted on their faces, so that in the interest aroused thereby, one could forget their homeliness. To be frank, they are mostly stupid persons, or at least apathetic. Whence, then, the beauty? Its source is twofold: in the artist's vision of his subject and in his technical rendering of what he found.

The secret of an artist's vision, when it is truly artistic, is that it is inspired by a feeling for beauty and is looking for beauty. He is not searching for something to represent, but for a means of expressing what

EQUESTRIAN
PORTRAIT OF
PHILIP IV

VELASQUEZ

THE PRADO

he feels of beauty. To such a one as Velasquez it matters little what he is called upon to paint. He is not aware of those limitations which the ordinary man calls ugliness. To him the subject is a manifestation of life and life to him is beauty in every one of its aspects, and to render that beauty is sufficient. And you may say that he finds life and the beauty of life not only in the face and figure, action and gesture, of his subjects, but in the clothes they wear and the accessories that surround them. All are contributory to the sense of life with which the subject inspires him, so that he extracts from fabrics and objects of still-life a raciness of character or subtlety of expression that lifts them above the ordinary and gives them the distinction of beauty.

But, after all, it is not so much a question of extracting beauty from the subject as of putting beauty into it. The final achievement is one of technique. There are hundreds of pictures which a layman can admire without thought of technique. Interest of subject predominates, or at least is sufficient to establish interest; charm of sentiment attracts, or splendor of color or composition. But Velasquez's compositions for the most part are studiously reserved; his color sober; scarcely the quiver of sentiment disturbs the equanimity of his subjects, and the latter, in the ordinary sense of the term, have no human interest. Such attractiveness, therefore, as they have, is almost completely what has been put into them by his technique.

Take, for example, the bust-portrait (p. 92) of *Philip IV* in the National Gallery, assuredly one of Velasquez's most notable achievements. How languid the pale hair; the face, how foolishly prolonged, flabby and expressionless! Imagine it painted by a second-rate artist, and you would pass it by. But before this portrait you pause and linger long. Why? neither you nor I can tell; except simply that we are in the presence of the mystery of life, so that even this sallow, puffed face attracts and rivets our admiration. Even a painter cannot tell you how it was painted. Its technique eludes him. Yet it is the technique which holds him to the spot. He *feels* that here the mystery of living structure and tissue has been compassed by the mystery of the artist's creativeness. Something of the same suggestion of spontaneously created plasticity is to be found in the beautiful child-portrait of *Don Baltasar Carlos* in the Metropolitan Museum, New York. Usually, however, the means by which the effect is obtained may be discovered. You note the character expressed in some detail of the canvas; and then approach until you see the brush strokes that produced it, no less magical because patently apparent. In fact, you find yourself let in behind the scenes of the artist's dramatic representation of facts and in a measure share the joy of creating the illusion.

It is a hopeful theory that out of one's limitations may grow one's greatest strength. And it is true of Velasquez. The very narrowness of his scope of actual vision encouraged a closer scrutiny. He discovered beauty in things which had escaped the notice of artists to whom larger liberty of choice was allowed. This is particularly revealed in his attitude toward color and light. The range of color-hues involved in the costumes of his royal sitters was restricted; blacks and greys prevailed, with occasional notes of rose or blue. Debarred from a variety of hues, Velasquez learned to see the variety of nuances which any one hue presents under the action of light. His blacks ceased to be merely the negation of color; they took on silvery hues, and sometimes brown ones. Even the bare drab wall of his studio became a field for the play of light. He grew to be an intimate student of the identity of the effects of light and color; noting how the "local hue" of an object varies in color-value according to the quantity, direction and quality of the light upon the various planes of its surface. Some artists before his time had noted this principle, but none until Velasquez and Hals—for it is a strange coincidence that the Dutch artist also was following this track—had given a practical application to it. Others had treated the local color, as if it were separate from chiaroscuro. They would model the form in monochrome and then spread their local hue over the whole in a thin transparent glaze which permitted the underpainting of shaded, half-shaded, and light parts to be seen through it. Velasquez actually modeled in the local color, by representing the differences of color-values that it assumed, according as the rise or depression of its surface caught more or less of light.

This, of course, is what other artists had done, notably Leonardo da Vinci in his *Monna Lisa*, Jan Van Eyck and Holbein in their portraits; but with a difference. They imitated each color-value as exactly as they could, modeling their surfaces with innumerable facets. Velasquez, like Hals, discovered for himself the principle of Impressionism; so far, at least, as this term is applicable to technical processes. For its meaning has become extended to include the artist's mental standpoint, so that to-day, when we speak of an impressionist, we mean one who in literature, or drama, or painting or sculpture colors his impressions according to the moods of his temperament. But in Velasquez there is nothing of the temperamentalist. He is the cool, impartial observer of objective facts. But, instead of seeing them, as Holbein did, in the multiplicity of their detailed variations, he saw them in the large. Primarily, that is to say, he aimed, not at perfection of parts, but at a unity of ensemble. To secure this he sacrificed the less important to the more important; eliminated the unessential and emphasised the salient. His mental process was one of keen analysis, directed to the question of what was and what was not essential, and also to the study of the relative degrees of importance which the essentials bore one to another and the whole. The end in view was to make the ensemble, not only organically simple, but an organic unit.

No doubt Velasquez was led to these results by his study of color and light. He not only discovered but made technical use of the fact that light tends to unify the colors and forms of objects; that it encompasses them and affects their contour lines, causing some to be sharp and others more elusive, and also, as we have noted, changes the values of their hues. Further, he became aware that under the action of light colors act and react on one another; that, for instance, the value of the flesh of a face will be affected by the color-light

AN ACTOR, CALLED 　　　　　　　　VELASQUEZ
"DON JUAN OF AUSTRIA"

THE PRADO

of the costume or of other objects near it. Thus, we ourselves may have observed how the white gown and face of a woman, seated on the grass, will assume values of reflected green. Or, if we are acquainted with the Lumière process of color-photography, we are familiar with the surprises of unexpected reflections which the camera records.

    All of these results of his study Velasquez employed to render the truth of sight and to unify the impressions. For it was the sum of the impressions he had received that he learned to render. He, in fact, formed in his mind a net impression of the whole scene, then translated each part into its proper share in the total of impression. It is a process which in the case of so great an artist as Velasquez is an act of high imagination, giving birth to an act of real creativeness. The result, then, is not an imitation of nature's truth but the new creation of an equivalent artistic truth; yet, with such an illusion of natural truth that it still meets his own ideal—"truth, not painting." Hence the stimulus which the spectator feels in the presence of his finest works. He is urged to be an active participator; to retranslate the equivalent of truth into the natural truth; to read from the shorthand of the brush strokes the full text of the longhand; to adjust his own eyes and mind to the reception of the impression and that a unified one. He becomes, in fact, a part-creator in the picture; somewhat as an intelligent spectator of a good play finds himself a part-actor in the dramatic situations.

. . . .

The story of Velasquez's life is little else than an enumeration of incidents in his career as an artist. He was born June 6, 1599, in Seville, where his father, Juan Rodriquez de Silva, a lawyer of an old Portuguese family, had settled. The mother was Geronima Velasquez. Hence the son's full name, Don Diego Rodriquez de Silva y Velasquez, was shortened according to Andalusian custom into the family name of his mother. His parents dedicated him to the study of letters and philosophy, but yielded to his desire to become an artist. After a short period in the studio of Francisco Herrera, he was placed under the care of Francisco Pacheco, an academic painter of no great merit, but a man of considerable learning, whose house was a resort of the most cultivated society of the city. The young Velasquez profited so well by these surroundings, that Pacheco accepted him as a son-in-law. He was married to Juana Pacheco in 1618, the result of the union being two daughters, Francisca and Ignacia, the former of whom subsequently married Velasquez's own pupil, Juan Bautista del Mazo. At this time, the School of Andalusia, under the influence of Ribera's pictures, was abandoning Italianate mannerisms in favor of the naturalistic motive. When the young king, Philip IV, ascended the throne in 1621, Pacheco began to scheme that his most promising pupil should be brought to the royal notice. A visit to Madrid was planned in 1622, and on this occasion Velasquez gained the notice of the Count-Duke de Olivares, the king's prime minister and favorite, who in the following year summoned him back to Madrid. Under the Count's direction and aided by his purse, Velasquez produced an equestrian portrait (which has disappeared) of the king, who was so well pleased with it that he took the young artist into his service. Thus, in 1623 began that mutual friendship of monarch and painter, which resulted in a close companionship of nearly thirty-seven years. It was interrupted only by the king's occasional journeys of state and by Velasquez's two visits to Italy.

In 1628 Rubens arrived as an ambassador extraordinary from the King of England. His visit was prolonged for nine months, during which he painted several pictures for the King. Velasquez was deputed to act as his escort in the visits which he paid to the Escoriál and to the royal picture galleries. He was thus brought into touch with the most renowned painter of the day at the period of his most splendid achievement. The association must have broadened the young man, but it did not cause him to falter in his own attitude toward nature and art. Rubens urged him to go to Italy and study the great masters, and the King endorsed the advice.

The first visit was made in 1629 under circumstances of importance. For Velasquez started in the train of the Marquis Spinola, the most renowned Captain-General of the age, whom he was to immortalize in the *Surrender of Breda*, and on his arrival in Italy presented letters from the Count-Duke de Olivares which procured him admission to the most famous galleries. He copied some of the works of Michelangelo, Raphael and Tintoretto, and brought back five original canvases: *The Forge of Vulcan*, *Joseph's Coat*, two views of the *Villa Medici* and a *Portrait of Doña Maria*. The first, notwithstanding its classic subject, is naturalistic. Velasquez has taken advantage of the story of Apollo announcing the infidelity of Venus to her husband, while he is at work with his assistants, in order to make a study of the nude form, as a vehicle for the expression of action and emotion. But the composition has nothing of the method of Italian idealism, while it abounds with charming passages of still-life painting, thoroughly Spanish. The Villa Medici studies are particularly interesting evidence of Velasquez's preoccupation with nature, even among the masters in Rome, and his serious regard for landscape, which forms an important feature in many of his portraits. His return to Madrid in 1631 marks the end of what is regarded as the first period of his career. The remainder is similarly divided into two parts.

The chief works of the first period beside those already mentioned are the early *Adoration of the Shepherds* (National Gallery), *The Lady with the Fan* (Wallace Collection), *The Adoration of the Kings*, *Los Borrachos* or *The Topers*, and *Philip IV. Young*, all of which are in the Prado.

Philip welcomed his artist back with new favors, appointing him to the post of Aposentador Mayor, whose duty it was to superintend the arrangements for the King's lodging during his excursions to the country. It was a means of keeping his friend with him, though it must have seriously interfered with the work of the artist.

An influence of the first Italian visit may be traced in the large decorative canvases which characterise the middle period. Olivares had presented his palace of Buen Retiro to the King, and the latter employed Velasquez and other painters to embellish it. Hence followed the equestrian portraits of *Don Baltasar Carlos*, *Olivares* and *Philip* himself, and the historical picture, *The Surrender of Breda*. In addition, this period produced the *Christ at the Pillar* (National Gallery) and the Prado portraits of *Philip IV as a Sportsman, Don Baltasar Carlos as a Sportsman, Don Fernando de Austria as a*

Sportsman, The Sculptor Montañéz, and the portraits of dwarfs and actors, among the latter the so-called *Don Juan de Austria* (p. 100).

Velasquez started on his second visit to Italy in June 1649, and returned to Madrid in the summer of 1651. It was on this occasion that he painted the portrait of *Innocent X*, which is now in the Doria Gallery in Rome. On his return home the King made him Marshal of the Palace, which entailed upon him the onerous duties of arranging court festivities. These, too, had encreased in frequency and pomp owing to the King's second marriage; this time with his niece, Mariana of Austria, a girl of fourteen. Notwithstanding such interruptions Velasquez produced during these last nine years of his life some of his finest works and his masterpiece, *Las Meniñas (The Maids of Honor)*. Among the other canvases are *S. Anthony Visiting S. Paul*; *Las Hilanderas (The Weavers)*; *Portrait of Queen Mariana* (p. 119); *Portrait of Doña Maria Teresa* (or *Margarita Maria*); *La Infanta Doña Margarita Maria*, of the Louvre; *Philip IV Old* (p. 92) and the *Venus* (National Gallery); *Æsopus*, *Moenippus*, *The God Mars*, The Dwarf called *Antonio El Inglese*, and the actor *Cristobal de Pernía, called Barbarroja*. All the above, except those otherwise specified, are in the Prado.

In June, 1660, the marriage, which had been arranged by Cardinal Mazarin between the young Louis XIV and Philip's daughter, María Teresa, was celebrated upon the Isle of Pheasants, in the little river which separates Spain and France on the West of the Pyrenees. The weight of the burden of preparation and supervision fell upon the Marshal of the Palace, and proved more than Velasquez could sustain. He broke down at the end of the ceremony and, returning to Madrid, died a few weeks later, August 6, 1660. His wife survived him only seven days.

. . . .

In a work of this scope it is impossible to go into the questions which have arisen over the authenticity of many of the pictures ascribed to Velasquez. For information on this head the reader is referred to the latest critical work on the subject—"Velasquez" by Señor A. de Beruete y Moret, and to the continuation of the subject by his son in his recent book, "The School of Madrid." Both are published in English. The net result of their study is that many of the pictures ascribed to Velasquez are either copies of Velasquez's work, made by his son-in-law and pupil, Mazo, or original works of the latter, who from constant companionship with Velasquez had learned to imitate his style so closely. Here, I will satisfy the curiosity of the reader only by saying that these critics pronounce the *Philip IV in Hunting Costume*, of the Louvre, to be a copy, and the *Admiral Pulido-Pareja*, of the National Gallery, an original, by Mazo.

By reference to a few examples, let us trace the evolution of Velasquez's way of seeing and rendering his subject. The earliest picture in the Prado is *The Adoration of the Magi*. This is assigned to about the year 1619, the probable date also of *The Adoration of the Shepherds* (National Gallery). Both, therefore, belong to the Seville period. Perhaps in the *Magi* we can detect something of the sophistication of the learned Pacheco, as well as the influence of the new naturalistic movement. The figures are naturalistic; while the grouping and lighting are artificial, academical. The light is arbitrarily centered on the Mother and Child; the shadows which envelop the other figures are also arbitrary; neither shade nor light is naturally distributed; the whole is a studio convention.

Velasquez finished *Los Borrachos*, (The Topers) in 1629, the year he sailed for Italy. It represents the climax of his development during the previous ten years, and what progress it exhibits! The distressing murkiness of the older picture has disappeared; the chiaroscuro in this is luminous; the flesh parts brilliantly lighted, the shadows warm and transparent. But it still presents the studio chiaroscuro, designed for the sake of the pattern and unity of the composition; the light and shade are not nature's. Wonderfully naturalistic, however, are the heads of these peasants, brimming with character and life. The men are engaged in a mock scene, in which a youth, playing the part of Bacchus, is crowning a comrade with vine-leaves. As Señor Beruete says: "The Spanish 'picaresca,' or rogue comedy, which plays such a brilliant part in the literature of that day, has never been better rendered than it is in this astonishing picture." But we note, in anticipation of the artist's further advance, that the picture presents only a pictorial ensemble, not yet a natural unity. It is a mosaic of splendidly executed items—faces, nude forms, costumes and still-life—each of which merits and indeed demands individual study. As a *pattern* the composition holds together as a unit, but it does not present a unit of *sight*. One cannot see it as a whole; the eye travels from point to point, resting on each and enjoying it separately. The picture is a masterpiece of its kind; but it is not of the kind that Velasquez at length achieved in the single, unified vision of *Las Meniñas*.

The Forge of Vulcan, which Velasquez executed in Italy (1630-1631), is remarkable, in the first place, for its freedom from the trace of Italian influence. Velasquez had come face to face with the giants, but had preserved completely his independence. Michelangelo and Tintoretto had shown him their capacity to express emotion and dramatic energy in the action of figures, particularly nude ones. Velasquez observes; but applies the principles to suit his own ideal of truth; no heroics, or pageantry of display; simply the natural expression of emotion, under natural circumstances. The workshop, the articles of still-life, the action of the men, have been studied from observed facts. Their work having been suddenly interrupted, each man pauses for a

LAS HILANDERAS (THE WEAVERS)   VELASQUEZ

THE PRADO

momment. How extraordinarily the arrest of action is suggested! Remark particularly the gesture of the three, who have suddenly halted in the sequence of their several hammer strokes. It is the figure of the god only that seems out of place and touch with the rest. It is disagreeably prettified, stiff and formal in gesture, with affected disposition of the drapery. It seems to be an academic solecism amid the naturalness of the scene.

    The second point of interest is that in this picture Velasquez shows the first marked feeling for tone. There is no brilliance here or richness of hues, such as make *Los Borrachos* glow like magnificent enamels. The color-scheme is very reserved; drab, relieved with white flesh, brownish black tools and armor and the golden-amber of Apollo's drapery. It shows the artist already feeling toward color as light; multiplying values rather than hues; studying the local hues in the variety of the light upon them, instead of applying to them an arbitrary chiaroscuro; even contriving to give to his whole scene a certain envelope of atmosphere. The figure, raised at the back, scarcely takes its proper place in the aerial perspective; otherwise the scene, barring the artificial halo of the god, represents an immense step in naturalistic expression.

    We pass to the superb equestrian portraits of the little *Don Carlos*, *Olivares*, and *The King*. I wish it had been possible to reproduce all three in these pages; for, while they are all superbly decorative, magnificently large in expression and thrilling with force, they represent differences of psychological feeling. That of the *Carlos*, the darling of the Court, is sprightly and lovable; *bravura* distinguishes the ostentatious pleasure-loving courtier-favorite, while a kingly gravity, tinged with the artist's affection, ennobles the *Philip* (p. 96). The boy bounds forward from the landscape; *Olivares* caracoles toward it, pointing to imaginary exploits; the King is placed athwart it, his figure quietly dominating space. How carefully Velasquez calculated this last effect is clear from the fact that two strips of canvas have been stitched on to the sides of the original piece. The artist evidently felt the need of more space to secure for the figure the required ascendancy. It was a frequent practice of his to add a piece to the top or sides of his canvas, which, as R. A. M. Stevenson, himself an artist, has remarked, throws a light on Velasquez's method of work. He does not appear to have made careful original studies of his subjects, a fact corroborated by the very few drawings that he left behind. He rather seems to have attacked his subject immediately on canvas, pushing it hotly forward to realise his mental picture, and then, if necessary, adjusting the size of his canvas to secure a final unity of feeling. For the same purpose also he sometimes changed the drawing, as he proceeded, painting over the original design which now frequently shows through. In this equestrian Philip IV, for instance, even the photograph will show how he has altered the disposition of the horse's legs, bringing them nearer together, as if he had felt that the more scattered positions detached from the quietude and dignity of the ensemble.

The horse in this portrait as compared with that of the *Olivares* is deficient in splendor of muscular action. It is more monumental, the brownish bay mass forming a magnificent support to the black armored figure, with its pale rose sash. Philip was justly regarded the finest horseman of his day. Observe the seat of the figure, how absolutely its action is adjusted to that of the horse. Note, also, that while the masses of the landscape support the horse's mass, the king's figure shows free against the spaces of dove-grey sky; his black beaver with its white and plum-colored plume lifting proudly against the white cloud. Compare this setting of the hat upon the head, with the respectively different treatment of the same details in the other two portraits. Each is psychologically related to its subject. Compare also the scintillating liveliness of the child's embroidered costume and fluttering scarfs, so birdlike in gaiety of plumage, with the sumptuous bravado of Olivares' gold-fringed, wine-red damask-silk bow, and his gold-striped armor—the whole effect intentionally a trifle *outré*. What a contrast of grave dignity in the King's damascened breast-plate, brown velvet, gold-embroidered breeches, greyish drab gloves, pale buff boots and deep plum-red sash that floats over the horse's stern! In the ensemble of concentrated, controlled stateliness the only flashes of accented energy are the horse's white fetlock and his superbly animated nostril and eye.

In his first period Velasquez painted an historical subject, *The Expulsion of the Moriscos from Spain*; but the picture perished in the burning of the Alcázar in 1734. The *Surrender of Breda* is therefore the only example of his work in this genre. It was executed after his first visit to Italy, where he had seen how Titian and Tintoretto utilised such subjects for palace decorations. Velasquez, true to himself, has tried to represent the scene as it actually might have happened, yet with certain formalities of balanced masses, to meet its decorative purpose. The picture, in fact, presents a mixture and, if one may dare to say it of a picture so famed, a confusion, of motive. The result is neither frankly an historical picture, such as Velasquez would have imagined it and rendered it, if his intention had been single; nor is it satisfactory as a decoration. The pattern of the composition is handsome. So too its coloring, which includes a lovely blue sky, fleeced with white; fainter blue and bluish-green and warm drab distance; blue coated troops in the middle distance; and deep sapphire blue in the squares of the flag on the right and in the breeches of the man whose white shirt shows against a black horse on the left of the center, and lastly in the costume of the man with a gun over his shoulder on the extreme left. The coat of the adjoining figure is brownish buff; the horse on the right, dark reddish brown. Spinola is clad in black armor, studded with gold; Justin of Nassau in brown and gold. All this is highly decorative, but not of itself sufficient to produce a decoration. For the secret of a decoration lies in the treatment of the planes, so that a sense of flatness may be preserved. There is nothing of that here; the bulk and depth of the foreground masses contradict it. The front figures of the man on the left and the horse opposite are alone sufficient to prevent a mural feeling. On the other hand, from the point of view of an historical picture, the attempt to treat the groups as masses, seen against the background, has resulted in a certain confusion of their planes, and in a general lack of interesting suggestion in their details. Only the treatment of the two principal figures is entirely satisfying. Nothing could exceed the beautiful expressiveness of the conqueror's noble condescension and the no less dignified humility of the conquered. To this, the heart and soul of the conception, the rest comes near to being but an ornamental and rather distracting surplusage.

Of the three sportsmen portraits, that of the *King* is again the finest. That of his youngest brother, *Don Ferdinand of Austria*, is a somewhat earlier work, painted, possibly, before the artist's visit to Italy; and the little *Don Carlos*, charming as it is, has lost a portion of its canvas (it is suggested that it may have been cut from its frame to save it at the time of the fire), so that the composition has not the consummate propriety and dignity of the King's portrait. The latter is also distinguished by the masterly discretion of its tonality, which is based on brown. The tree trunk is brown; the foliage brownish olive; the cap and doublet lighter tones of the same and the trunks and gaiters darker; the gun, light brown and the glove drab brown; the dog, orange-tawny. Thus the figures and tree count as one handsome mass, in which the predominant spot is the pale face, set off by the soft, blond chestnut hair. The sleeve of the undercoat is black and silver, forming a thread of minor emphasis to connect the head and the gloved hand, the latter so full of character and technical distinction. The background of landscape is composed of a stretch of tawny drab grass, sloping up to bluish trees, seen against a grey sky, curdled with cream.

A fine example of the numerous portraits of dwarfs and actors, is that of the buffoon, nicknamed *Don Juan de Austria* (p. 100). The figure is shown in a drab grey interior, from which a door opens on to a view of sea-shore and a burning ship. The costume is of black velvet and a peculiarly subtle pale claret-colored silk. The expression of the man is one of concentration, to the suggestion of which every part of the figure so curiously and completely contributes its share, uniting in a perfect ensemble of feeling. In the atmospheric envelope and extreme choiceness of color this canvas is a worthy prelude to the masterpieces of the final period.

. . . .

To one of the latter allusion has already been made: the *Philip IV* of the National Gallery. How infallibly just is the placing of the black bust and head against the dark background! With what *finesse* have been calculated the accents of the chain and ornaments and collar, in order to secure and at the same time alleviate the emphasis of the empty, solemn head with its puffed, waxy features and soft, pallid hair! How absolutely a unit is the whole impression! while the brush work is the *ne plus ultra* of impressionistic technique.

A miracle of painting also is presented in the portrait of a child, identified variously as *Doña Margarita* or *Doña María Teresa*, and in that of the not much older *Doña Mariana de Austria*, Philip's second wife

LAS MENIÑAS (THE MAIDS OF　　　　　　VELASQUEZ
　　　　HONOR)

THE PRADO

(p. 119). The child's "guarda-infante" is of cloth of silver, woven diagonally with pale rose silk, all ashimmer with veiled lustre. Vermilion bows adorn her waist, a jeweled rosette of the same color her corsage, while a small rosette under the left ear and a plume on the right of the head, both vermilion, set off the soft straw-colored hair and the fresh tender hues of her face. Curtain and carpet are a rosy crimson, thus completing a tonal scheme of exquisitely delicate vivacity. In the second portrait the Queen's robe is of black velvet, shot with brown, decorated with silver bullion. Notes of poppy scarlet appear at her wrists, while a pale scarlet mingled with silver is the color of the plume and of the ribbon flowers in her hair. The curtain, in color pale rosy burgundy, frames a dark olive background, a concavity of atmosphere, in the half-light of which appears a dainty gold clock upon a table. These two canvases are marvels of technical achievement and surpassing loveliness. A head and bust-portrait of this Queen, apparently in the same costume, hangs in the Metropolitan Museum, New York.

A broader method, in which one strongly feels the exhilaration of the brushstrokes, is represented in the *Æsopus* and *Moenippus*. The grizzled black hair and pallid features of the former show against a warm drab-olive background. In the lower right corner is a spot of black and creamy fabric; opposite to it a creamy colored bowl; otherwise the figure is a study in browns of peculiarly fine quality. The background of the *Moenippus* is somewhat colder than the *Æsopus*; in key with the black cloak. The cap, boots, and the table and pitcher are of tones of brown; the beard is grey and the flesh of the face ripely rubicund. Even in the photograph one can appreciate the masterful breadth of the draperies, and feel through the modulation of the values the bulk of the figure beneath.

The *Venus* of the National Gallery, if it is to be reckoned among the works of Velasquez, is his only example of a female nude. While it attracts at first, it subsequently proves disappointing. In the emptiness of the back it is hard to recognise the hand of the master, who in early days modeled so skilfully the man's back in the *Forge of Vulcan* and whose modeling generally is so masterly and full of interest. Nor can we easily reconcile with his unerring truth of observation the drawing of the reflection in the mirror, which instead of being smaller than the real head is somewhat larger. Moreover the red of the curtain and general color scheme lack the choiceness and subtlety of the canvases of the latest period, to which the *Venus* is assigned.

We reach now the two celebrated masterpieces: *Las Hilanderas*, (*The Weavers*), (p. 109) and *Las Meniñas*, (*Maids of Honor*) (p. 114). They are very different. Both are triumphs alike of science and of inspired vision; yet, by comparison, I should distinguish the *Maids of Honor* as a miracle of vision, the other as a marvel of science. For we may be conscious of the science in the one and lose thought of it entirely in the other. In *Las Meniñas* the unity of the ensemble seems as artless as the scene depicted; in *Las Hilanderas* it is perhaps less complete, certainly less simple and seems to suggest the consummate knowledge needed to achieve it. The interest of the former pervades the whole chamber and centers in the little princess. That of *Las Hilanderas*, seems, at least at first, to be distributed into three parts, and the focus point for the eye—Where is it?

Studying the two pictures, as is possible in the Prado, since they hang upon the same wall, near enough for the eye to travel backward and forward from one to the other, one discovers, I believe, that the problem involved in each is the reverse of that of the other. *Las Meniñas* shows a partially lighted interior, with the chief light on the little figure in the foreground; while the problem of the other picture is a dimly lighted, or rather darkened foreground, and a fully lighted background. In *Las Hilanderas*, in fact, the artist's chief motive was the alcove, pervaded by a clear light that illumines the blues, greys and pale rose of the tapestry. Velasquez had seen it so and realised how the effect was heightened by the dimness of the spot in which he stood. Conscious of this, one begins to understand that the focus point of this picture is the shaded dull-red figure in the center of the middle distance. But it is a focus point of departure; not, as in *Las Meninas*, designed to draw our attention to it, but to direct it to the lighted space behind. When once we have recognised this, order begins to establish itself in what seemed to be the divided interest of the canvas. The beautiful figure, on the right, of the girl in a white chemise no longer holds our attention too exclusively. We see in her the artist's twofold purpose of explaining the front plane of his scene, and pointing through the shaded figure to his main motive. We have discovered the proper view of sight; it is in front of this girl, looking diagonally toward the alcove, and the group on the left is introduced to balance the composition. Yet even now, after one thinks one has captured the secret of the unity of the ensemble, so cunningly achieved, the beautiful figure of the girl on the right of the foreground may arrest our interest and distract it from the whole. It is because of this, that for my own part, there seems to be more of science than of inspiration in this vision.

Not so with *Las Meniñas*. Here one forgets to analyse—there is no need to do so—one simply accepts the scene and feels its consummate truth. How consummate it is, only familiarity with the original can reveal. It is a truth that grows upon the consciousness, stimulating it to demand more and yet more difficult tests of its truthfulness, and satisfying every one. And the unity which is the secret of the truth has not been obtained by monotony of hue. The canvas is alive with color, strong notes of most vivacious hue. The Princess's dress is creamy silver with a bunch of rose on her breast. This rosy note is echoed in varying tones: in the glass that is being presented to her; on the artist's palette; in the curtain reflected in the mirror at the back where the King and Queen appear; in the bright cuff ribbons on the silvery grey dress of the maid-in-waiting on the right, and in the dull rose costume of the child on the extreme right. The dwarf next to him wears a dress of slaty blue, decorated with silver; the kneeling maid, a greenish grey upper dress over a skirt of deep greyish green, and Velasquez himself is in black. But

DOÑA MARIANA DE AUSTRIA   VELASQUEZ

THE PRADO

the mere enumeration of the colors gives no idea of their positive vivacity, as they show out brilliantly in the light, and none of the marvellous realisation of the textures. Nothing has been evaded; nothing seems to have given the artist a moment's pause or difficulty. Yet, when all is said, the greatest marvel is the concavity of the drab-grey room, filled with luminous atmosphere; clear, around the foreground figures, but with infinite nuances of clearness, melting into varieties of penetrable mystery in the receding perspective. In the whole scene not a trace of evasion or confusion! Everything is readily comprehended, because rendered with immediate precision, as if in a moment of infallible improvisation.

Las Meniñas was not only the matured achievement of Velasquez's long research into the effect of light upon color and upon their relations to one another in space; it was a new kind of picture. It is composed, built up of light. According to older conventions of composition the large space above the figures would be considered empty. But here it is not empty; it is filled with tones of light, with luminous aerial perspective that balances the group of lighted forms below. Possibly the photograph may not convey this impression to one who has not seen the original. But in the presence of the latter there can be no doubt of it. The upper part is as full of material as the lower; we may even find it more beautiful, because so infinitely subtle and stimulating to the imagination. Never before or since has the truth of natural appearances been so marvellously rendered, or the beauty of every day truth been so heightened by the artist's inspired imagination. *Las Meniñas* is an apocalypse, the revelation of a supreme vision.

In the decline of Spanish art and the general interest of Europe in Italianate and rococo motives, Velasquez during the eighteenth century was forgotten. Toward the end of that century, however, Goya derived inspiration from his works, and nearly a hundred years later Manet, Whistler and others rediscovered him. His example has been the chief influence in leading the world back to regard a painting as a work of art, and in teaching the painter himself the technique that will entitle it to be so considered. The duration of his influence has corresponded with the vogue of naturalism which has prevailed in Literature and the Fine Arts, a reflex action of the general scientific attitude of the time. The vogue is passing, and Velasquez's immediate *influence* may grow less. But his *reputation* will endure, because it is founded upon the lasting foundation of "truth, not painting."

CHAPTER VII

MAZO

A TWOFOLD interest attaches to Juan Bautista de Mazo, the pupil and son-in-law of Velasquez. In the first place, he was employed by his master to copy many of the latter's pictures, so that he is involved in the controversies which have arisen over their attribution. Secondly, he was himself an original portrait painter, and practically the only representative of landscape painting in the Spanish School.

Mazo was a native of Madrid, the date of his birth being placed approximately in 1612, because he is reported to have lived a little over fifty years, and his death took place in 1667. It is not known when he entered the studio of Velasquez, but he married the latter's daughter, Francisca, in 1634. The King signalised his approval of the marriage by relieving Velasquez of his duties as Usher of the Chamber and transferring them to Mazo. The young people made their home with their parents-in-law, and Mazo worked in constant companionship with Velasquez until the latter's death. He seems to have had a remarkable faculty of imitation, for Palomino, writing shortly after Mazo's death, says: "He was so skilled as a copyist, especially with regard to the works of his master, that it is hardly possible to distinguish the copies from the originals. I have seen some copies of his, after pictures by Tintoretto, Veronese and Titian, which are now in the possession of his heirs. If these copies were produced in Italy, where his talent is unknown, they would be taken without any doubt for originals." Velasquez utilised this ability of his pupil, as Rubens and Rembrandt made use respectively of theirs, to assist him in part or in whole. Copies of his pictures were required by the King for presentation to members of the Royal Family of Austria, to ambassadors and others to whom he wished to show special favor. In some cases Velasquez himself made a replica, more often, because of the interruptions of his Court duties and the stress of other work, would employ Mazo to make a copy, leaving it intact or touching it up as the case might be.

An example of one of these copies, according to Señor Beruete, is the *Philip IV as Sportsman*, of the Louvre. He assigns it as a copy, made by Mazo, of the original that is now in the Prado. There is a slight difference between the two. In the Louvre picture the King holds his cap with the left hand on his hip; in the Prado the cap appears upon the head. This was an alteration, subsequently made by Velasquez, for one can still trace in the original picture a dark mass over the hip, where the under-painting shows through. The copy, therefore, must have been made before the alteration.

An example of an original by Mazo, which has passed as a Velasquez, is, according to Señor Beruete, the celebrated portrait of *Admiral Adrian Pulido Pareja* in the National Gallery. It is signed with the name of

DOÑA MARIANA DE AUSTRIA						MAZO

THE PRADO

Velasquez in Latin. But the Spanish critic points out that, while a signature itself is no proof of authenticity, this one differs in matter and character from the only other three instances of the signature of Velasquez on a picture. These are on undoubted works of the master: the full-length *Philip IV* in the National Gallery, the portrait of *Pope Innocent X* in the Doria Gallery, and the fragment of a picture which is preserved in the Royal Palace in Madrid. Studying the technical qualities of the *Admiral* and comparing them with those of undoubted examples of the same period in Velasquez's career, Señor Beruete reaches, in brief, the following

- 82 -

conclusions. The figure does not stand firmly on its feet; the latter and the legs are badly shaped; the hat looks like a sack; its curve is prolonged by that of the left arm and both are parallel to the curve of the body; the hands are poorly modeled; the baton is held without distinction, the silhouette of the whole figure is neither sure nor beautiful, and the masses lack just disposition and balance. The whole is without the distinction, sureness of touch and *brio* that characterise all the authentic portraits of Velasquez. It is a fine work by a painter of less power than Velasquez, but bears so strong a resemblance to his style, that it can be by no other than his pupil, Mazo. For other pictures, hitherto supposed to be by Velasquez but now claimed by Señor Beruete for his pupil, the reader is referred to the Spanish critic's book: "The School of Madrid."

With the *Portrait of Doña Mariana of Austria* (p. 122), the second wife of Philip IV, we reach an unquestioned original by Mazo. It is the same subject as in Velasquez's portrait (p. 119), only the girl-bride has now become a girl-mother. Her child, the Infanta Margarita, about four years old, appears in the rear with attendants and a dwarf. It is a drab interior rather reminiscent of that in *Las Meniñas*. The crimson curtain and chair and the Queen's pose, on the other hand, recall Velasquez's portrait, just mentioned. The suggestion, in fact, throughout is Velasquez, but not the handling and the style. Compare, for example, the hand on the chair in the one portrait and the other. In the Mazo there is an absence of modeling and character. How characterless also the line of the right arm, and wanting in decision and distinction the whole silhouette of the figure. Yet the picture has a very great charm of refinement and tender feeling.

Another probable original by Mazo in the Prado (No. 1083), *Portrait of Prince Baltasar Carlos*, is attributed to Velasquez in the official catalogue. It is one of a number of similar attributions that surprise the visitor to the Prado. The portrait in question shows the Prince, now in his fourteenth year, standing with his left hand upon the back of a chair, while his right hangs gracefully, holding a plumed hat. The figure is entirely in black against a drab background. There is no picture by Velasquez, known to exist, from which this could be a copy. That it is not an original by the master is evident in the softness an indecision of the drawing, and the actually bad drawing of the right leg which does not connect properly with the hip. It is therefore assumed with probability to be an original by Mazo, and the fault of drawing is explained by the fact that he was only twenty-four years old when he painted it. This picture has an undeniable elegance, but falls very short of Mazo's *Doña Mariana* in accomplishment.

However, both the originality and the capacity of Mazo are best displayed in his landscapes, which have now been collected into one of the upper galleries of the Prado. As we have noted, Mazo is the single great landscape painter of the old Spanish School. While the contemporary School of Holland, in the persons of Ruisdael, Van Goyen, Hobbema, Cuyp and many others, was developing landscape as an independent branch of art and carrying it to a high level of representation and expression, the Spanish School, with the exception of Mazo, still used it in subordination to the figure. Considering that both schools were influenced by the naturalistic motive, how is one to account for this difference? Probably in the fact that, while the Dutch artists were in a great measure painting to please themselves and choosing their own subjects, the Spanish artists worked directly under the patronage of Royalty and the Church. Portraiture and religious subjects were the only work demanded of them. Added to this may be the fact that the Dutch ideal was democratic, the Spanish aristocratic. The Dutch people were interested in themselves and in the everyday concerns and environment of their lives, and the Dutch artists, being of the same stuff as their public, contributed to the popular taste. On the other hand, both the Spanish monarchy and the Church were strongholds of aristocracy and both had close affiliations with Italy, the art of which had been pre-eminently aristocratic. It was based, as has been pointed out in a companion volume to this one, "The Story of Dutch Painting," on the idea of the superiority of the individual person, or, translated into terms of art, on the supremacy of the human figure as an art-motive.

We may well believe that Mazo was encouraged in his feeling for landscape by Velasquez himself. For it is recalled that the latter during his leisure in Rome painted two vistas in the gardens of the Villa Medici. There is also in the Prado a *View of the Arch of Titus*, which the catalogue admits was probably painted in Spain from a sketch made in Rome. Later criticism, however, has concluded that it was Mazo who painted this from Velasquez's sketch, and has also assigned to the younger man several other landscapes, originally supposed to be by Velasquez. In this judgment the Director of the Prado acquiesces, for the pictures have been placed in the gallery devoted to Mazo's landscapes.

Before considering them, let us note the contribution made by Velasquez, indirectly through his portraits, to the art of landscape painting. He used landscape, with the freedom and feeling of one who comprehended it and loved it, in his equestrian and sportsman portraits, in the *Surrender of Breda* and particularly in one of his latest works, *S. Antony Visiting S. Paul*, where the figures are small and the picture is virtually a landscape subject. The chief distinction of all these landscape scenes is that Velasquez, the student of light, has brought natural light into the scenes, in which respect they differ from the landscape of Italian backgrounds, even those

THE FOUNTAIN OF THE TRITONS   MAZO

THE PRADO

noble ones of Titian's, which are pervaded with what is, comparatively speaking, a studio lighting. Velasquez is in a sense even more naturalistic than his contemporaries, the Holland masters of landscape, for, although they rendered nature more intimately, they were disposed to translate the actual hues of nature into a tonality of their own. Velasquez, on the contrary, recorded what seemed to him to be the facts of sight. He, therefore, reappears among the moderns of the nineteenth century, in landscape as in portraiture, one of themselves, because their mutual study was the light of nature.

One of Mazo's most important landscapes, known to be his by documentary evidence, is the *View of Zaragoza*. It hangs in the Velasquez gallery of the Prado, because the master added the figures which are distributed in three planes throughout the foreground. But the river beyond, dotted with sailboats, the bridge and distant view of the city are unquestionably by Mazo. The silvery deep olive-green of the water and the accurate definition of the buildings, which nevertheless are felt as masses, recall the finest manner of Il Canaletto, while the suggestion of light in the sky is more naturalistic than the Venetian ever attained. It is a picture that interests one to compare with the single landscape of Jan Vermeer: his *View of Delft* in the Hague Gallery. Each gives one an extraordinary realisation of the actuality of the scene; but, while the Holland artist's picture breathes an intimate domesticity, the work of the Spaniard is psychologically different, suggesting a certain *hauteur* and exclusiveness; partly, no doubt, through the introduction of the choice groups of figures by Velasquez.

The three landscapes originally attributed to Velasquez, but now included by the Director of the Gallery among Mazo's are: *The Fountain of the Tritons* (p. 122), *Calle de la Reina de Aranjuez*, and *The View of Buen Retiro*. In the first named the tree-stem on the left-foreground, sprinkled with leaves, is reminiscent of Velasquez, and the beautiful little figures, so suggestively rendered, may have been added by him. But the handling of the grey-green foliage of the further trees, softly blurred against a bluish grey sky, is unlike the method of Velasquez as seen in any of his landscape backgrounds. On the other hand, the soft faint masses of tone, subsequently worked over with little curly strokes, can be found to a greater or less extent in the foliage parts of all Mazo's landscapes in this room. The latter, it should be observed, vary in subject, including views of buildings, romantic scenes of rocks and waterfalls, sea-shore in combination with cliffs and temple-ruins, and views more simply naturalistic. To each the artist has adopted a technique suitable to the occasion, so that it is not at first sight easy to recognise them as the work of one man.

Mazo, in fact, in his approach to landscape, shows nothing of the timidity and indecision and tendency to follow closely his master, such as characterise his portraits. Here he shows himself an original experimenter, freely pursuing his own motive. In the case of *The Fountain of the Tritons* it has brought him to a method that anticipates the impressionistic style of Corot. The peeps of sky through the soft screen of trees; their very coloring, the single tree-stem in the foreground and the envelope of cool grey atmosphere—Corot might have painted them.

The *Calle de la Reina* has again a strangely modern air, somewhat that of a Jules Dupré, when he is not stirred to emotional effects. The avenue, leading to the palace of Aranjuez, recedes in the shadow of tall trees, which tower up in dark masses against a fine twilight sky. Its light is dimly reflected in the grey-blue water of a shadowed lake on the left of the foreground; the rest of the latter being enlivened with figures which form the retinue of two arriving coaches. All these sprinkled forms count as dark spots upon the pale-lighted sandy road. In its truth of observation and simple nobility of feeling this landscape would do honor to any school of any period.

To assist his appreciation of Mazo's romantic and mythological landscapes, the visitor to the Prado will do well to step into an adjoining gallery, devoted to the works of Claude Lorrain and Nicolas Poussin. It is true they are not represented here at their best; yet perhaps sufficiently well to suggest the character of their work and certainly its spirit. Particularly in the case of Claude Lorrain it is slighter, shallower than the spirit of Mazo's corresponding scenes; less reinforced by close observation of nature; or, it may be, inspired by softer influences. For the source of the difference is perhaps the contrast of character of the Spanish as compared with the Italian landscape. Mazo has noted to good purpose the stirring cloud effects that pile high above the gaunt sierras, and their grandeur and bigness have inspired his feeling. By comparison, the mellow skies of the French-Italian landscapes, seem trivial, and communicate their slighter feeling to the formal, classically composed foregrounds, so that they seem mannered. In Mazo's on the other hand, the grandeur of the sky's suggestion spreads to the mountains, rocks and water, investing the whole with a sense of structural power and therefore of sincerity. In fact, in these romantic, mythological subjects Mazo stands alongside Turner rather than Claude and Poussin.

CHAPTER VIII

CARREÑO

AMONG the painters who were contemporaries of Velasquez and after his death helped to stem for a little while the decline of the School of Madrid, special notice is due to Juan Carreño de Miranda. He came of a noble family of the province of Asturias, his father being Alcade de los Hijosdalgos or Chief of the Council of Nobles, in the town of Aviles, where Juan was born in 1614. When he was still a boy he accompanied his father to Madrid, and made up his mind to be an artist. His father, at last acquiescing, placed him with Pedro de las Cuevas, who had also been the teacher of José Leonardo and Pereda. Carreño afterwards worked with a painter, Bartolomé Roman; but by the time that he was twenty years old had so distinguished himself that he was entrusted with several important commissions. Velasquez recognised his talent and, thinking he should be employed in the King's service, commissioned him to paint some frescoes for the royal palace. These were destroyed in the fire of 1734.

In 1669 Carreño was appointed one of the Court Painters, a post which he continued to hold after the succession of the young king, Charles II, when the regency was in the hands of the Queen-Mother, Mariana de Austria. In this capacity Carreño executed portraits of the royal family which represent his best work.

Meanwhile his popularity was based upon his decorations and altar-pieces. His decorative ability, which had been recognised, as we have seen, by Velasquez, included a familiarity with the technique of fresco painting, a branch of the art which had few representatives among Spanish painters. The taste for it had been introduced by the Italians summoned to decorate the Escoriál, and perpetuated by other foreigners who were employed in decorating the principal churches and convents. From them Carreño acquired a knowledge of the process. He seems (for I am not acquainted with Carreño's mural decorations) to have been distinguished in his use of it by a combination of Italian decorative composition with types and motives characteristically Spanish, and by very delicate and spiritual schemes of color.

Perhaps the character and quality of the latter may be discovered in the altar-piece by this artist in the Hispanic Museum, New York. It is a *Conception*; the subject being presented in the usual way prescribed by the Church. But the composition is looser, if one may say so, than Murillo's in similar pictures, with lines more flowing and masses distributed more gaily. It is the arrangement, in fact, of a painter accustomed to the liberty of decoration on a large surface. It has a sweep and elegance that make it akin to the compositions of Antolinez and particularly of Cerezo, whom we briefly discussed in the fourth chapter. In its color-scheme also, it favors theirs. All these artists, in fact, represent

CHARLES II   CARREÑO

THE PRADO

a reaction from the more sober and restricted color-schemes, imposed upon Velasquez and other Court painters. At the same time, they are characteristic of the decline which had already begun. The coloring of this *Conception* of Carreño's is distinguishably prettified; pearly pinks and blues, soft greys and greens, perilously suggestive of the *bonbonière* style. And the sentiment of the whole is correspondingly suave, almost, if not completely, to insipidity. Similarly sentimental are this artist's *Magdalen in the Desert* in the Academy of San Fernando in Madrid, and his *San Sebastian* of the Prado.

The Magdalen looks like a matured Ariadne, abandoned by her lover. She is posed upon a rocky seat, so that her beautiful arms may be seen to advantage and the long line of her graceful figure duly emphasised. Meanwhile she lifts her tearful gaze to the sky, at a carefully calculated angle that will impress the beauty of her neck upon the sympathetic spectator. As for the *San Sebastian*, it should make a gentle lady weep to behold how this tender body has been abused. In fact, the student who has discovered the true sources of greatness in the Spanish School of painting will not take Carreño very seriously when he is in these moods. Fortunately for his present reputation there is a graver and more dignified side to his art.

In his portraits, especially those of the members of the royal family, Carreño shows himself to have absorbed no little of the influence of Velasquez. These portraits of Charles II and his mother, Queen Mariana, vary in quality; for he was called upon to repeat them, and the replicas display a lack of interest and falling off in technical distinction. Perhaps the handsomest portrait of the King, painted when he was still a lad of twelve, is the one in the Kaiser-Friedrich Museum, Berlin. The boy, as usual in a black velvet suit, with long blond cavalier locks descending over his shoulders, stands resting his left hand on a marble-topped table, which is supported on a lion and ball pedestal. His face has not yet acquired the expression of settled melancholy and is gracious and lovable. The coloring is rich and luminous, and the concavity behind the figure, full of atmospheric suggestion. The replica of this in the Prado is tighter and drier in treatment, lacking in quality of tone and lighting.

Another portrait of this period, showing the figure at half length is owned by Señor Beruete. Judged by the photograph of it, reproduced in his "School of Madrid," it is a very superior canvas, distinguished by graciousness and dignity. It is a terrible contrast to turn from the weak yet winning beauty of the boy to the portrait in which Carreño has depicted the man (p. 132). In all the range of portrait-painting can we find a face so degenerate as this? The face droops to an inordinate length, as if the vacuous brain could no longer hold it in position; the mental distortion is reflected in the grotesquely exaggerated features; the expression of the pallid mask is one in which hope and joy of life are extinguished and reasonless fear is habitually present. Such was the last of the proud Hapsburg line of Spanish Sovereigns.

Carreño's most important work, however, is the *Portrait of Queen Mariana of Austria*, in the Munich Old Pinakothek, of which there is an unsatisfactory replica in the Prado. But the Munich portrait, once seen, impresses itself indelibly on the memory. It is a cold, implacable indictment. The surly sadness of the girl-wife, painted by Velasquez (p. 119), who had our sympathy for the cruel grossness of her lot, has hardened into callous obstinacy and weak self-indulgence. Her widowhood has brought authority without a sense of responsibility, she has betrayed her maternal trust in order that through her child's feebleness she may hold on to power; she has dallied between her lover and confessor, and is now *devote*. Clothed in black and white weeds that resemble a nun's garb, she sits squarely at a table, a loveless, forbidding woman. Yet strangely haunting because of Carreño's analysis and fearless exposition.

CHAPTER IX

RIBERA (LO SPAGNOLETTO)

THOUGH recognised as the leader of the School of Valencia, José or, as he is sometimes called, Jusepe de Ribera spent most of his life in Naples, where his Spanish pride, combined with his somewhat diminutive stature, procured him the sobriquet, *Lo Spagnoletto*. He was born in 1588, eleven years senior to Velasquez, in the province of Valencia, in the hill-town of Jativa, the cradle of the Borgia family. Hence the proud title which he often appended to his signature, "Spaniard of Jativa." His parents, Luis de Ribera and Margarita Gil, took him to Valencia that he might study Latin with a view to becoming a man of letters. But José, even thus early showed his independence by declaring that he would be an artist, and was accordingly placed under the care of Francisco Ribalta. The latter, we recall, was the link of transition from Italian mannerism to the native naturalistic schools of Valencia and Andalusia; at one time producing thinly painted subjects of extravagant sentimentality, at another showing himself quite masterful in naturalistic representation. This blend of naturalism and sentiment, the latter frequently carried too far, distinguishes also the work of Ribera and through his influence many artists of the Andalusian School, Murillo in particular. The naturalistic tendency is Spanish, common to North and South alike; the sentiment is a bias given to it by the Southern temperament.

While still a youth Ribera made his way to Rome, where his handsome face and evident ability attracted the notice of a cardinal, who took him into his house and would have cared for him that he might pursue his studies in comfort. But José, nothing if not independent, found the restraint irksome and went back to his rags and poverty, declaring that he needed the stimulus of necessity. He made copies of some of the Raphaels and the Caraccis in the Farnese palace, and even found means to visit Parma and Modena and study the works of Correggio. But the pictures which most attracted Ribera were those of Michelangelo Caravaggio, who worked in Naples. So to Naples he went, although he had to leave his coat behind in Rome to pay his boardbill. Whether Ribera actually studied under Caravaggio is uncertain. Anyhow, since the latter died in 1609, the association could not have lasted more than a short time. Meanwhile, even if Ribera never saw Caravaggio in the flesh, he could not escape his spirit. It was a part of the turbulent atmosphere of the Naples of that day, into which with a violence, equal to Caravaggio's, the independent young

Spaniard was quick to fling himself. Fortune favored him, for a rich art dealer gave him some commissions and, discovering his ability, determined to attach him to his own interests. He offered him his daughter's hand in marriage, and Ribera, having experienced the stimulus of poverty, was now resolved to taste the encouragement of wealth and ease, and accepted it. Soon after his marriage he produced a life-sized picture of the *Martyrdom of S. Bartholomew*, who was flayed alive. The ghastly scene was represented with such horrible naturalism, that when the picture was exhibited outside of the art-dealer's shop, a crowd gathered about it. This attracted, as no doubt it was intended that it should, the notice of the Spanish viceroy, the Duke of Ossuna, whose palace window overlooked the spot. Having learned the cause of the excitement he sent for the picture and was so impressed with it that he bought it, appointed Ribera his painter in ordinary, and gave him apartments in the palace. Thus, almost at a bound, Ribera found himself upon the topmost rung of the ladder. He was rich and now courted by the richest and most powerful, who presumed that he had the ear of the viceroy. In artistic circles the young artist had taken the place of Caravaggio and invested it with still greater honor. He was the recognised leader of the naturalists in their war of extinction with the Eclectics.

It is necessary to note the rivalry between these two contemporary schools, since it throws a light on an extraordinary episode in Ribera's career. With the death of Tintoretto in 1592 the last of the giants of the Renaissance had passed away. They were succeeded by a race of pigmies, who strutted in the mantles of Raphael and Michelangelo. They are called "Mannerists," differing, however, from the Mannerists of Spain. For while the Spanish imitated the great masters in order to acquire the secrets of their greatness, at the same time, as we have seen, infusing the result with something of the raciness of the Spanish character, the Italian "Mannerists" aped the past in an attempt to galvanize it into continued living.

The "Mannerists" soon become obscured by the "Eclectics," whose headquarters were in Bologna, the home of the Caracci. For the school grew out of the influence of the five brothers Caracci, especially the three, Annibale, Ludovico and Agostino, who led the way in what was to be a "revival" of art. Its principle was a catholic eclecticism, which should combine the drawing and power of Michelangelo, with the color of Titian, the grace and sentiment of Raphael and the soft dreamy chiaroscuro of Correggio. The movement spread throughout Italy, being variously represented by the Caracci, already mentioned, Domenichino, Guido Reni, Guercino, Sassoferrato, Carlo Dolci and others of more or less merit. Whatever may be thought of these painters individually, it is scarcely to be denied that the principle underlying their art had in it nothing of original growth. It was dishing up the past, instead of providing meat for the present.

Meanwhile, outside of the "Eclectics," the spirit of the present was asserting itself in a reaction from Classicalism to Naturalism—to use a hackneyed term, in a return to nature. That the stronghold of the Naturalists became Naples, which was under Spanish rule is a significant fact. It was an instance, by no means single, of the Spanish influence reacting upon Italy. The movement however was started by the Italian Caravaggio, a man of impetuous temperament and possibly coarse tastes, who by way of bringing the Bible story into touch with every day life, peopled his sacred scenes with personages drawn from the slums of Naples. How great a painter he could be upon occasions is shown in that handsome canvas in the Dresden Gallery, *The Card Players*. However, the style usually associated with his work and that of his followers is one of violent types and exaggerated dramatic energy. The "Naturalists" were also addicted to the use of dark shadows, which gained for them the nickname of "Darklings." Between them and the "Eclectics" there was perpetual rivalry, waged with that intensity which only Latin peoples can put into an artistic controversy. On the part of the Neapolitan naturalists it was war literally to the knife, for they did not scruple to employ the bravo and his stiletto in their efforts to hold Naples against the enemy. It was to the leadership in a fight of this sort that the young Ribera succeeded, and he went into it with an unscrupulous ferocity that has left on his memory the blot of a very discreditable episode.

The Chapel of St. Januarius in the Cathedral of Naples was to be decorated. A cabal was formed between Ribera, a native Neapolitan, Giambattista Caracciolo, and a painter of Greek birth, Belisario Correnzio. The last named had already made so bitter an attack on Annibale Caracci that the latter had been driven out of Naples. The three now determined to secure for themselves the decorating of the chapel. The commissioners at first assigned the work to one, Cavaliero d'Arpino, who had been Correnzio's teacher. He was assailed with persecution, and forced to take refuge in the Benedictine monastery of Monte Cassino. Then

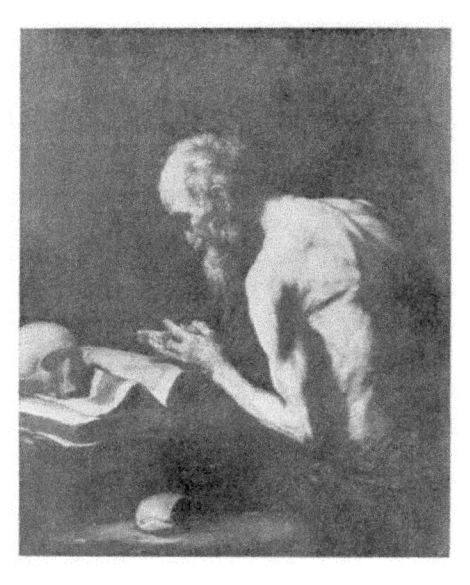

HERMIT SAINT   RIBERA

THE PRADO

Guido was selected. Two hired bravos set upon his servant, thrashed him, and ordered him to tell his master that a similar fate was in store for himself should he begin the decoration of S. Januarius. Guido fled the city; and his pupil, Gessi, was chosen as a substitute. He arrived in Naples with two assistants, who were inveigled on board a boat in the bay and never seen again. The commissioners now yielded and gave the commission to the triumvirate. But a little later they revoked the order and offered Domenichino a handsome remuneration, with a promise of protection, if he would undertake the work. He consented and became immediately the target of an insidious persecution. Threatening letters were sent to him; his character was slandered and his ability as a painter impugned; the plasterers were bribed to mix ashes with the mortar on which his frescoes were to be painted; and finally Ribera prevailed on the viceroy to order some pictures of Domenichino. These were carried from his studio before they were finished, or retouched and ruined before reaching the viceroy. At length, in despair, Domenichino fled to Rome; but was induced to return and shortly afterwards died under suspicion of having been poisoned. The cabal, however, failed of its purpose. The Neapolitan died the same year as Domenichino; the Greek two years later and Ribera painted only one altarpiece for the chapel, *The Martyrdom of S. Januarius*. The decorations were executed by one, Lanfranco.

For his share in this disgraceful intrigue, and because of his being a foreigner, Ribera incurred the hatred of a large number of Neapolitans. To this, probably is to be attributed the story which passed into a tradition, that Don Juan of Austria, while on a visit to Naples, induced Ribera's daughter to elope with him; and, soon growing tired of his victim, placed her in a convent. In consequence of shame and grief, Ribera, so the story goes, sank into a profound melancholy, until one day he left his home and was never again heard of. This is now believed to be a mere fabrication of Neapolitan hatred; the true facts being that Ribera settled down to a life of honor and prosperity and finally died in Naples in 1656.

. . . .

In the popular imagination Ribera is associated with pictures of martyrs and ascetics, with scenes of cruelty and suffering and the portrayal of old and wasted bodies. The impression is justified, for the taste of his time demanded these revolting subjects, and Ribera's own temperament made him more than acquiesce. He represented them with a zest that proves he revelled in his opportunities. But this is only one aspect of Ribera, and even in itself not complete, for it is prone to take no account of the superb artistry with which he invested the unpleasantness of these themes.

Thus, in the example, selected for reproduction here, because it is characteristic of Ribera's best known subjects, the original has a beauty which in the reproduction may possibly escape observation. The head of this *Hermit Saint* is of extreme nobility both of technique and expression. In the suggestion of the powerful skull, the boldly modeled flesh and the clustering masses of grizzled hair and beard, there is an unusual feeling for and realisation of the dignity of human form. It is not merely that the artist has selected a model with a fine head, and rendered its benign and grave distinction, but he has heightened the expression by the expressiveness of the technique. The artist's sympathetic imagination and extraordinary reverence, not for the saint-idea in his theme but for humanity in its relation to art, have informed the technique with a noble sympathy, grand imagination and a sovereign reverence. For the point, difficult to put into words, is that technique such as this, while it is magnificent as mere representation, achieves the higher quality of expression, and the measure of the latter is the quality of the artist's conception not only of his subject but even more of his art, as one of the noble mediums of expression. So, in the presence of a work like this, the spectator forgets his dislike of the subject and finds his imagination kindled and his capacity of abstract appreciation heightened. Even the Saint's back though you may not believe it from the photograph, which has reduced the transparent shadows to opacity and robbed the flesh of its glorious luminosity, adds its quota to the stimulus of the intellectual-esthetic sense. For, in this capacity, not only to delight the sense perception but to stimulate also the intellectual conception of beauty in the abstract, Ribera belongs in the company of Velasquez. He occupies a lower rank because his art, like himself, was less self-centered and controlled; more dependent upon subject and at the mercy of his own impetuous temperament. In the art of both naturalism was lifted mountain-high; but, while Velasquez was the summit, aloof, unapproachable, Ribera is the torrent, racing, often madly, to the valley. Yet in its career there are level pools of quiet pause, and it is these that the general estimation of Ribera has overlooked.

I am not thinking of his portrayals of the *Immaculate Conception* or his *Assumption of the Magdalen* in the Academy of San Fernando. These are rather examples of the concessions that Ribera was obliged and perhaps willing to make in the direction of obvious beauty. They satisfied the Spanish taste in female loveliness, but have little abstraction of expression; and are inclined to be sentimentally pretty. It is rather when you visit the gallery in the Prado devoted to Ribera's works, that you experience a new impression of this artist. With the exception of a powerful but ghastly *Martyrdom of S. Bartholomew*, the general suggestion of the gallery is the reverse of the violent and sensational. A sense of grave dignity prevails, which one begins to discover is largely the result of a fine reserve and frequent subtlety in the color schemes. For example, there is a canvas of life-size figures, representing the Holy Trinity. On the Father's knees lies the limp form of the Christ. It is grievously disfigured with grossly naturalistic blood stains; but one gradually loses the insistence of this in admiration of the elevated beauty of the picture as a whole. The Father's head, benign and tranquil, is seen against a sky in which are faintly discernible the flocking heads of cherubs. From his shoulders floats a silvery plum-colored drapery, while a mantle of pale rose, lined with violet, lies over the shadowed lapis-lazuli of the under robe. It is a color scheme of choice splendour, full of subtle stimulus to the intellectual-esthetic imagination.

A very interesting canvas is the *S. John the Baptist in the Desert* for the feeling of it is pagan, a trait rarely met with in the art of Spain, which had so rigorously opposed the Humanistic movement. The figure, nude nearly to the waist, is that of a shepherd youth, with large smiling mouth and eyes glancing to one side. The face sets one to thinking of the so-called *S. John the Baptist* of the Louvre, attributed to Da Vinci. The Ribera has something of the faun-like suggestion; only it is less subtle, piqueing less to mystery;

the suggestion being rather of wild, young animal life, a creature of silent, vacant places, not afraid yet watchful. The figure is at the foot of a big tree-trunk, a red drapery covering the upper part of the legs and the stone on which it is seated. The arms are extended; one aloft, holding a staff, the other lowered to feed a lamb; both forming pliant loops which increase the suppleness of the whole design. In its blend of classical and naturalistic composition and feeling, and the character of the thought which prompted it, the canvas is probably unique in the Spanish School as an example of the direct influence of Humanism.

One turns to a *Penitent Magdalen* (Prado, 980), not to endorse her very lady-like sentiment, but to admire the way in which the beautiful brown hair is rendered and the exquisite color and texture of the old-rose drapery. A similarly choice treatment of this delicate color, shot with silver light and dove-grey shadows, appears in *Isaac Blessing Jacob*. Then for another fine example of color one may note a half length, *S. Simon*. Here again is a head of magnificent character; black hair and beard, ruddy features, massive brow, a characterization, generously masculine and vigorous. A warm brown drapery hangs over the slightly yellow-tinted brown of the robe, which shows below it the collar and cuff of a grey shirt; all this placed against a dark olive background. The tonality, organised with extreme delicacy, is in its ensemble superb. Another choice passage of color occurs in *S. Bartholomew*, where the saint is shown, life size, seated beneath a cliff. He holds across his body a white drapery; or such is your first impression of the hue. But study reveals a more subtle tissue of smoked ivory and grey, woven into the pallor of the white.

However, the finest example of Ribera's subtle vein of color-expression in this gallery is in the *Jacob's Ladder*. The sleeping figure reclines horizontally across the foreground, a hand supporting the head, while in the sky are faint suggestions of ascending and descending angels. The foreground consists of slabs of rock out of which, at the back of the figure, rises a tree-trunk, with a broken limb. The figure is clothed in an olive-greyish-brown habit, resembling a monk's; the hair and beard are black in strong contrast to the pallor of the face, which is slightly flushed with warmth and puffed with sleep. The suggestion of sleep is, indeed, rendered with extraordinary truth; it seems no idle fancy that one hears the breathing and watches the stir of the drapery over the rise and fall of the chest. But the dignity of this canvas depends upon the color scheme, cold, severe, constrained; so opposite to the sensuous, impassioned or splendid; yet withal so stimulating to the imagination. This picture is a grand example of the intellectual-esthetic quality in Ribera's finest work; placing this artist far above the estimate popularly formed of him. It is not difficult to discover the influence of this large, grave feeling in the earlier work of Murillo and in almost all the work of Zurbarán.

CHAPTER X

MURILLO

THE most popular artist of the Spanish School is unquestionably Murillo. He was the idol of his contemporaries in Andalusia; most admired by connoisseurs and public in the eighteenth century, and, although during the nineteenth century artists and connoisseurs have extolled Velasquez and more recently Goya and El Greco at his expense, to the popular taste Murillo is still in the ascendant.

There must be a good reason both for the depreciation of Murillo on the part of artists and for the continuing appreciation of the public; therefore one must try to discover them impartially. For, while the popular estimation of any particular artist at a given period is apt to be wrong—perhaps more often wrong, than right—it scarcely can hold its own through the chances and changes of over two hundred years without having in it some considerable element of right. What then is the abiding something in Murillo's art which makes this perennial appeal? For my own part, I believe that, if you can sum it up in a word, it is the spirit of Youth.

One imagines Murillo (not without plenty of justification for the idea) as a man who, in a psychological sense, never grew old; retaining to the end the naiveté and simple faith of a child. He continues, therefore, to appeal to adults who have kept something of their youth with them or to those whose study of art has not passed beyond the stage of instinct. For, just as it is possible for a man to have matured understanding and appreciation of a work of art, and yet be like a child amid the intricacies of an electric power-house, wondering, admiring, but without capacity to estimate the value of this plant as compared with another; so a man may be full of knowledge, even to the length of sophistication, and still exhibit the naiveté and unreasoning appreciation of a child in the presence of a work of art. Necessity or chance determined that he should cultivate his higher mental powers in another direction; art is to him only an occasional distraction; his feeling toward it is regulated solely by his instinct. As he would say himself, "I know what I like."

To tell such a man that he is wrong would be not only cruel but false. From his own standpoint he is not wrong; he is very much in the right, if the end of art is the heightening of a man's nature through contemplation of the beautiful. This thing is beautiful to him, and through the beauty he sees in it he finds his nature refreshed, purified and enlarged. What more could you advise for him at that particular stage of his artistic development? It is true to the standpoint of his own instinct. Would you have him substitute your standpoint for his? Are you sure that your own leads to any better results for you than his for him? Anyhow, unless he changes his standpoint through convictions that have grown into his mental consciousness and been endorsed by his experience, his last state may be worse than the first. He was honest and sincere before; now he may be only a glib repeater of borrowed preferences.

. . . .

Bartolomé Estéban Murillo was born in Seville in 1618, probably on the first day of January. The official catalogue of the Prado begins its reference to the artist's career with the following significant words:

"When this great artist came into the world, his parents, Gaspar Estéban Murillo and Maria Perez, were living in a humble house in the Calle de las Tiendas. It was but three months since the Virgin Mary, in the mystery of her Immaculate Conception, had been proclaimed the patroness of the Dominions of Philip IV. Under such happy auspices was born the *Painter of the Conceptions.*"

This dogma of the Conception, which for centuries had occupied the minds of theologians and scholars and captivated the imagination of the faithful, was nowhere held in greater honor than in Spain, and the center of the cult was Seville. Meanwhile, the authority of the Church, as expressed in Councils and Bulls, had maintained a neutral attitude toward the question. When, however, at the end of 1617, Paul V, yielding to the repeated urging of the Crown and Church of Spain, issued a Bull which forbade teaching or preaching in opposition of the dogma, the joy of the Spanish people was profound. Seville herself celebrated the glad tidings in a frenzy of religious rejoicing. A magnificent ceremony was performed in the Cathedral and amid the strains of choir and organ, salvoes of artillery and a

MIRACLE OF THE LOAVES AND   MURILLO
FISHES

MOSES STRIKING THE ROCK

HOSPITAL DE LA CARIDAD, SEVILLE

pæan of the bells of the cathedral and churches, Archbishop de Castro swore to maintain and defend this peculiar tenet of his see. It was followed by a splendid entertainment in the bull-ring, where in the presence of enormous throngs the nobles appeared, accompanied by magnificent retinues, and one in particular, Don Melchior de Alcázar, attended by his dwarf and four gigantic negroes, performed prodigies of valor and dexterity. It was recognised that a new era had commenced; that the old dark days of inquisitorial rigor were passed and love and gentleness were to reign henceforth. It was into this atmosphere of sweet religious ecstasy that Murillo was born, destined to become the artist who best succeeded in expressing it.

    Murillo's only teacher was his uncle, Juan de Castillo, who gave his pupil a thorough grounding in drawing, though his own style could not do much to help his pupil's advance in painting. After a time Juan moved to Cadiz and his nephew, without father or mother, was left to face life alone.

He gained a living by painting "bodegones," or still-life subjects, and pictures of saints, which he sold in the *feria* or weekly market. His ambition was to study in Rome and, as a first step, to visit Madrid. Having saved a little money, he made his way on foot to the capital and presented himself to his fellow townsman, Velasquez. The latter received him kindly and obtained permission for the young man to paint in the royal galleries. Here Murillo studied and copied the works of Titian, Rubens, Van Dyck, Ribera and Velasquez himself, to such purpose that the last-named advised him to go to Rome. But Murillo, who had now been three years away from Seville, determined to return thither. The same independent spirit which had enabled him to shift for himself and to leave home and study in wider fields, now assured him that he had gained what he needed without further travel. From the various influences which he had experienced, he discovered a style for himself. He returned to Seville without friends or influence, but opportunity presented itself. The monks of the convent of S. Francis wished their cloister decorated. Murillo applied to them for the commission. They would have preferred a well known artist of the city, but, having little money to offer, engaged the young, unknown painter. Murillo spent three years on this work, and, when it was completed, found himself the most famous painter in Seville. He had taken something from the several styles of the artists he had studied and imprinted upon it his own individuality. This expressed itself particularly in an ability to give reality to his picturing of the story involved in the legends of S. Francis. He had proved himself to be a great illustrator.

This term to-day perhaps involves a certain depreciatory significance. Men are often illustrators because they cannot find a market for their easel-pictures; or, having obtained a reputation as illustrators, are ambitious to be painters. The fact is, that illustration to-day is confined to books and magazines, and from the publisher's point of view is designed rather to attract attention to the text than to illuminate it. But in Murillo's day, as in Raphael's, illustration was a noble and honored art, the readiest and most efficient way of bringing the sacred truth home to the minds of the unlettered masses, and permitted so grand a scope, that it was also a decoration to monumental buildings. Thus the value of an illustration at that date, while it incidentally might be decorative, depended primarily on the appeal which it made to the hearts and understandings of the people. Murillo was a sincere Catholic; he could feel his subject in accordance with the Church's teaching, and moreover he had the gift of telling the story in the vernacular; depicting it in familiar guise and investing it with those touches of everyday life that pique and hold the interest of the simplest mind.

To be indifferent to the genius and value of such a gift is to admit oneself a careless student of human nature. It is either that we refuse to be interested in what interests the masses, or that we underrate the virtue of the latter being thus interested. To-day, in our modern experience, there are thousands of illustrators; but if one looks back, say, twenty years, how many are there who have been leaders, in the sense that they have caught the spirit of the age for the first time and given it an expression which the educated and unlearned alike recognise as something vital? This is the point. For the thousands who can perpetuate a tradition, imitate somebody else, or carry on the accepted convention, there will be found but one or two who can synthetise the time-spirit into a new expression. And for the worth-while of doing this? I repeat that, to-day, illustration is mainly a method of amusing vacant minds. But it was not so in the seventeenth century, any more than during the early and the great days of the Renaissance. It was something that influenced the lives of millions in their attitude to what, then at least, was of supreme moment, religion. Therefore, to estimate the genius and value of Murillo's gift of illustration we must not judge it from the standpoint of to-day, but in the light of the needs and desires of his contemporaries. Then we shall realise that what Murillo did for the simple, religious folk of Seville is akin to Raphael's contribution to the mingled Humanistic and Christian needs of Rome. Both were great illustrators, whose subject matter was religion, and who told their story in the medium that appealed to the sympathy and understanding of the largest number of people of their day. But the very freedom from Humanistic influence which characterised Murillo's art encreased its value to the people of Seville. It was essentially Spanish in its naturalism and specifically Andalusian in its sentiment.

. . . .

Murillo's method of painting has been described as exhibiting three styles—cold, warm and vaporous. According to this arrangement, the first style (*estilo frio*) is distinguished by cold coloring and dark shadows; the second (*estilo calido*) by warmth of coloring, stronger contrasts of luminous light and shade, and by increased plasticity of form; the third, (*estilo vaporoso*) by the vaporous or misty effects of atmosphere, enveloping the whole or part of the composition. But while his works show this variety of method, they cannot be distributed into periods, definitely characterised by one or another style. Nor will it repay the student to try to docket the different pictures according to any such pigeon-hole

SS. JUSTA AND RUFINA   MURILLO

PROVINCIAL MUSEUM, SEVILLE

system of division. He will rather become aware that, as Murillo attained to facility and confidence in his own way of rendering his intentions, he perfected his pictorial representation both of the naturalistic motive and of the spiritualised conception, which in whole or in part for the time being occupied his imagination. In some pictures you find the naturalistic motive either predominating or in complete control; in others it is combined with the spiritualised motive; while again, particularly in the *Conceptions*, the spiritualised intention is exclusively apparent. Whether it satisfies your own spiritual sense is another matter.

Nor can these varieties of motive be assigned to special periods of Murillo's career. For example, after he had established his reputation as a painter of *Conceptions*, he executed the series of works for the Hospital de La Caridad, in Seville. Two of these are produced on page 150. They were selected because they redounded to the reputation of Murillo in his lifetime, and yet exhibit a weakness which more or less is evident in all his works of illustration.

Neither the *Miracle of the Loaves and Fishes*, nor *Moses Striking the Rock*, contains any spiritual suggestion; for to the modern imagination at least the figure of Christ in the one and those of Moses and Aaron in the other seem to be invested only with a little symbolical distinction. Further, even the significance of the events is not suggested. If you take away the Christ, whose importance in the composition is already belittled by the group of women on the right, is there anything in the action of the figures and the expression of their faces to indicate that they are witnesses of a miracle? The scene becomes nothing more than a huge picnic, conducted on an absurdly meagre commissariat. So too, in *Striking the Rock*—where is the hint of the agony of thirst or of high-wrought emotion at the miraculous deliverance? But for the two central figures, whose impressiveness, such as it is, is confined to themselves, the incident might be simply that of a party of people gathered about a spring. To myself a very suggestive indication of the shallowness and insincerity of the whole conception is the introduction of the small boy on the sleek plump horse. It is a mere studio device for getting a spot on which to concentrate the light and for lifting one figure above the line of the others.

Another example of this series of Hospital subjects is the very famous *S. Elizabeth of Hungary*, now in the Prado. The scene is being enacted in the shadowed arcade of an imposing classical building. The saintly Queen, attended by two young ladies, charmingly attired, is washing the scalp of an urchin, who leans over a silver basin. A beggar sits on the ground removing a bandage from a festering sore, and a boy, with an expression on his face of exasperated distress, scratches his head and chest. Meanwhile an old woman sits looking up in worshipful gratitude at the face of the queen, who possibly returns her gaze. For she is turning her head away from the business in which she is engaged, as well as she may, since the head she is bathing shows a disgusting sore. Perhaps you may say that such details are incidental to a clinic, and may quote the example of Rembrandt's *Clinic of Dr. Tulp*. But the latter is frankly a naturalistic picture in which the cadaver forms the explanation and focus of the group of eager, intellectual heads, absorbed in the instruction of the master-surgeon. But Murillo's is an academically disposed composition, involving splendid classical accessories. It is, in the manner of its form, idealised according to the Italian tradition, while in its details grossly naturalistic. Yet Théophile Gautier, moved to a characteristic burst of sentiment, exclaims—"In his picture of S. Elizabeth Murillo takes us into the most thorough-going reality. Instead of angels we are here shown lepers. But Christian art, like Christian charity, feels no disgust at such a spectacle. Everything which it touches becomes pure, elevated and ennobled, and from this revolting theme Murillo has created a masterpiece." This begs the question which still remains:—Is the reality in this case so rendered, that it becomes "pure, elevated and ennobled"? The answer will depend upon the individual student's temperament and intellectual attitude.

This picture, indeed, and many others in the Prado arouse a suspicion which becomes more pronounced, when we visit the Museum and the Church of the Hospital de La Caridad in Seville, that, after all, Murillo was not so great a naturalist as he is credited with being. His Street urchins, such as appear in the National Gallery, Dulwich Gallery and the Munich Pinakothek are vigorous transcripts of nature, racy with Sevillian character; but in the *Holy Family*, called *Pajarito* (little bird) of the Prado, one discovers already a weakening of the naturalistic grip. The types are local, and the scene, as the mother stops in the winding of her thread to watch the child playing with a dog, while the father holds him tenderly, is such as might be enacted in any happy home of the people. But why the voluminous yellow mantle spread in graceful folds over Joseph's knees? It is a recollection of Raphael that has inspired this solecism in the everyday naturalness of the scene. Similarly, in one picture after another of Murillo's you can find the realities of the scene sacrificed to the picture-making devices learned from the Italians. Frequently, as in the *Vision of S. Antony of Padua*, and corresponding subjects, the miraculous nature of the incident gives a plausibility to these formal designs, which I venture to believe is lacking in the *S. Elizabeth*, *Loaves and Fishes* and *Striking the Rock*.

Nor is much of the nobility of the Italian method reproduced in Murillo's use of it. Too frequently its stateliness is invaded by a homeliness which borders on the commonplace. One finds little or nothing of the aristocrat in Murillo's equipment. He views his subject with the naiveté of an untutored mind and represents it with a simple disregard of anything that might lift it above the commonplace. And this is practically as true of his technique as of his mental approach. There are beautiful passages of color scattered through his works; fine rendering of textures, and precious *morceaux* of still-life. But his color-schemes are regulated by temperament rather than by knowledge and calculation; his brush-work is rarely distinguished and his chiaroscuro frequently has grown blackened with time. It would be impossible to view one of his acknowledged masterpieces beside even a work of secondary interest by Velasquez, without realising at once the hopelessly unbridgeable gulf both of mentality and execution that separates them.

In fact, it is not until one comes to his *Conceptions*, that Murillo acquires distinction. In these he shows an originality of idea, to which he has moulded for himself a suitable technique. He has learned to preserve the plasticity of form and yet invest it with a suggestion of being impalpable, and also buoyant, so that it floats of its own lightness. The arrangement of the subject, even to the colors, was prescribed by the

Church; being founded upon the vision, recorded in Revelation XII. 1. "And there appeared a great wonder in Heaven; a woman clothed with the sun, and the moon under her feet, and upon her head a crown of twelve stars." It is Murillo's triumph that he dematerialized the concrete suggestion; created about the figure the luminousness of unearthly light and, while he took for his model a girl of the people, invested herself and her angelic surroundings with the imagined reality of a vision. This, it is needless to add, represents a triumph of technique. In these subjects Murillo proved himself a superior and original painter. As to the quality of feeling expressed in them opinions may differ; but it can scarcely be questioned that it is emotional rather than spiritual. There is nothing in it of soul ecstasy, as in El Greco's visions; it is the sweet, rapturous sentiment of the warm-blooded, emotional South. The *Conceptions*, in fact, are the most characteristic product of the Andalusian School and the highest achievement of Murillo.

In conclusion let me quote the observations of the French critic, C. E. Beulé, concerning that portrait of Murillo's which he painted of himself when he was in the flush of youth with all his possibilities before him. "We find him brilliant, ardent, fresh-colored, the warm blood flowing close under his skin; his eyes black, penetrating, full of fire and fuller still of passion; his forehead high, and modeled with those slight bosses which show a quick but rather feminine intelligence; the lower part of his face (as is frequently the case with his countrymen) less finely cut, and marred by a coarse mouth and the heavy outline of the chin. The total impression is that of a nature in which ardor serves instead of force, a facile but superficial rather than profound intelligence, and, as a prime trait, highly mundane and sensual. Are not these the very qualities we find written in his works?"

Murillo's end was brought about by a fall from a scaffold. He lingered for a short time, spending his days in contemplation of Campaña's *Descent from the Cross* in the Church of Santa Cruz. He died on the third of April, 1682, and was buried, in accordance with his request, beneath this picture.

CHAPTER XI

CANO AND ZURBARÁN

ALONZO CANO was born in Granada in 1601. He belongs, however, to the School of Andalusia, for he studied in Seville and lived there until his thirty-sixth year. His teachers in painting were Juan de Castillo, the master a few years later of Murillo, and Francisco Pacheco, in whose studio Cano was a fellow-pupil of Velasquez. He also practised architecture and sculpture. Indeed, it was in the latter art that he particularly excelled and gained his first distinction. His teacher had been the celebrated Martinez Montañés, whose instruction was supplemented by the opportunities of studying the antique marbles collected by the Dukes of Alcalá, in their palace in Seville, the *Casa de Pilatos*. The influence of this training is perceptible in his best paintings which are characterised by excessive refinement of drawing and expression. Yet Cano's own nature was inclined to violence and lawlessness. Having fought a duel with the painter, Llano y Valdés, and wounded him, he found it convenient to leave Seville and settle in Madrid.

Cano, now in his thirty-sixth year, was kindly received by Velasquez and introduced by him to the Count-Duke Olivares, who employed him in his palace of Buen Retiro. Philip IV expressed a wish to see the newcomer's work and, being favorably impressed with it, gave Cano the appointment of drawing-master to the young Prince Baltasar Carlos, and later made him one of his own painters in ordinary. After some seven years of success Cano's stay in Madrid was terminated as abruptly as his sojourn in Seville. His wife was murdered. According to the artist's own account, he had returned home to find her dead in bed, clutching a lock of hair and pierced with many wounds, inflicted, apparently, with a pocket-knife. Her jewels were missing and the Italian servant had disappeared. Suspicion was at first directed against this man; but when it became known that the artist had lived on bad terms with his wife, while carrying on an intrigue with another woman, he himself was suspected of the crime. Whether guilty or not, Cano was alarmed for his safety and, giving out that he had left for Portugal, fled East to Valencia. Here he took refuge in a monastery, executing works for many of the neighbouring communities. At length, trusting that the affair had blown over, he returned to Madrid and sought asylum in the house of his friend, the Regidor, Don Rafael Sanguineto. He was, however, arrested and condemned to the ordeal. Pleading his profession as a painter, he was permitted to submit his left hand to the torture and, passing through it without a cry, was adjudged innocent.

Six years later Cano, desiring to settle in his native city, Granada, obtained through the King's influence the post of minor-canon in the Cathedral, with the proviso that he should be excused from his choral duties if

APOTHEOSIS OF S. THOMAS AQUINAS   ZURBARÁN

PROVINCIAL MUSEUM, SEVILLE

he took orders within a year. He endeavored to conciliate the very natural objections of the Chapter by executing some sculptural embellishments for the Coro. He also worked for the convents of the neighborhood and for private patrons, with one of whom he came into collision respecting the price to be paid for a statue of *S. Antony*. The man, who held the office of auditor of Granada, had demurred at the sum asked for a work which had occupied the artist only twenty-five days; whereupon Cano, anticipating Whistler, retorted, "You are a bad reckoner; I have been fifty years learning to make such a statue in twenty-five days." Then he dashed the *S. Antony* to the ground and smashed him. This was a sacrilegious offence that might have brought the artist under the jurisdiction of the Holy Office, but the auditor, instead of reporting the matter to that body prevailed on the Chapter to declare Cano's seat vacant because he had not according to agreement taken orders. Cano appealed to the King who obtained for him from the Bishop of Salamanca a chaplaincy which entitled the holder to full orders, while at the same time the Nuncio consented to grant him dispensation from saying Mass. So Cano returned in triumph to Granada, but never again would execute any work for the Cathedral. Indeed, it was in works of charity that the last years of his life were chiefly spent. He was so impoverished by them that, when he was stricken with his last sickness, the Chapter voted five hundred reals to "The Canon Cano, being sick and very poor and without means to pay the doctor"; and a week later added another two hundred reals to buy him "poultry and sweetmeats." He died on the third of October, 1667.

The Capilla Mayor in the Cathedral of Granada is enriched with sculptural works by Cano's hand and with some paintings. These represent the "Seven Joys of Mary," *Annunciation, Conception, Nativity, Presentation in the Temple,* and *Assumption*. They are placed so high, that from the floor it is very difficult to see them, while, even when you view them from the nearer approach of the triforium, the colored glass of the windows interferes with their effect. As far as one can judge on the spot and with the aid of photographs they are too flimsy in character for the monumental structure which they are intended to decorate. That this conclusion is correct appears probable when you study Cano's smaller altar-pieces. Some of them are painted so thinly, with so little variety of values of hue and so little interest of surface, that they seem to be empty. On the other hand, his best works, such as the *Mother and Child* over the Altar of Bethlehem in Seville Cathedral, and the *S. Agnes* of the Berlin Gallery, are so exquisitely refined that they need to be seen at close range.

The former is regarded as Cano's masterpiece. The type of the Virgin is of Granada, touched with Moorish warmth, a little more womanly and much more refined than Murillo's. But, like the latter's and like Raphael's Roman Madonnas, it is beautiful only in a physical and emotional way; it has nothing of the spirituality of El Greco's creations, so absorbed in the mystery of their sacred and miraculous estate. Yet among the Madonnas of the Southern artists there is probably none so pure in its loveliness and so lovely in its purity as this one of Cano's. A similar quality of exquisitely fragrant maidenhood appears in the S. Agnes. Both this and the other canvas represent sentiment, raised to the highest pitch of elevated feeling; yet remaining sentiment. I make the point because Cano, no more than the other Spanish artists, for all the religiosity of their pictures, touched the soul of religion. The only artist of the Spanish School to do this was the alien, El Greco.

. . . .

Francisco de Zurbarán was born in 1598 in the little town of Fuente de Cantos in the province of Estremadura. His father, a small farmer, convinced of his son's talent for drawing, took him to Seville and placed him under the teaching of Roelas. But there is little or no trace of this painter's influence in Zurbarán's style. In a general way the latter came under the spell of Ribera and Caravaggio; indeed, at one period of his career Zurbarán in consequence of his dark shadows was nicknamed "the Spanish Caravaggio." But you cannot become acquainted with Zurbarán's various subjects without realising that he owed his style chiefly, almost entirely, to himself; that he had shaped it to the needs of his own temperament. He was an out and out naturalist; in a sense the most conspicuously naturalistic painter of the Spanish School. For there is an austerity in his point of view, which separates him from the sentiment of Murillo, the passionate virility of Ribera and the aristocratic distinction of Velasquez. Zurbarán consorted with Monks; took advantage of occasional opportunities of retiring from the world into the quiet of a monastic community; and in the simplicity and frugality of his tastes was at heart a monk. The bare walls of a cell or refectory, the plain habits of the brethren, and the orderly formality of their lives, were more to him than subjects for his brush. They were so in tune with his own instincts, that he derived from them inspiration for his art; affecting not only his habit of seeing but his technique. Both became characterised by largeness and simplicity and by more or less severity.

These qualities are represented in the great altarpiece, *The Apotheosis of S. Thomas Aquinas*, executed when Zurbarán was only twenty-seven years old and generally considered his masterpiece. It is to be seen to-day under very favorable conditions in the Provincial Museum of Seville, for it is hung high in a good light and can be viewed from various distances. These advantages of placing no doubt count in the impression, differing so widely from the usual circumstances under which the altar-pieces of Spain are to be studied. But the impression received of the *S. Thomas* is that, with the exception of the *Funeral of Count Orgaz*, it is the noblest ceremonial picture that one has met in Spain. It is due to the magnificence of its organic simplicity and bigness, which give the composition an emphasis and carrying force. And what is true of the large masses, viewed from a distance, is equally true on a nearer view of the details. The latter resolve themselves into finely treated surfaces of drapery and particularly into the punctuating emphasis of keenly

MIRACLE OF S. HUGO   ZURBARÁN

PROVINCIAL MUSEUM, SEVILLE

characterised heads. The altar-piece was painted for the Church of the College of S. Thomas; whose founder, Archbishop Diego de Deza is represented below; kneeling opposite to the Emperor Charles V, who presumably had been a patron of the foundation. One has but to look at the reproduction of this picture (p. 163) to feel sure that all the heads are portraits; that of S. Thomas, "The Angelic Doctor," being, tradition says, a portrait of the Prebendary of Seville in Zurbarán's time. While each head is individualized, it is interesting to note how they are assembled into generic groups; the monkish type represented in the archbishop and his attendants; the man-of-the-world in the Emperor's group; the type of the thinker and spiritual leader in the four doctors of the Church, Gregory, Ambrose, Augustine, Jerome. Nor is there any less distinction of character in the S. Paul and S. Dominic, in the right upper corner. It is less manifest, however, in the Christ, and scarcely to be found in the figure of the Virgin. Two other points may be noted, as helping to explain the magistral impression of this canvas. In the first place, the effect of wide-openness in the upper part of the composition, where the clouds of glory are thronged with cherub heads, is carried down into the lower part by the view of the street, seen at a distance and dotted with intentionally minute figures, so as not to interfere with the emphasis of the groups in the foreground. The result of this continuance of lighted space is to create a unity in the composition, binding into an ensemble the three tiers of figures. Again, it is remarkable with what a comprehension of large, structural principles, Zurbarán has distributed the masses, respectively, of the plain and of the embellished draperies. The purpose of the whole pageant is to glorify S. Thomas and incidentally the Dominican order. The key and climax, therefore, of the whole is S. Thomas's black and white habit. To secure its emphasis the cardinal's red and the rich copes with their sumptuously embroidered orphreys have been massed about it. Meanwhile a portion of this enrichment is repeated below in the archbishop's robes and the emperor's cloak, and more faintly in the figures in the clouds. Here too S. Dominic supplies an echo of the black and white, which in turn are massed in the lower foreground. It is this fine ground-work, distribution and climax of black and white, which more than anything give this composition so noble a distinction: a certain chaste, choice, austere dignity.

Near this picture in the Provincial Museum of Seville hangs another fine example of Zurbarán's originality of composition; *The Virgin Blessing Various Monks*. The white-frocked brothers are kneeling in two groups, left and right of the central figure of the Virgin. She stands robed in delicate rose, with her arms extended, each hand on the head of a monk. Meanwhile her blue mantle, fastened at the throat with a magnificent jewel, is held suspended by two cherubs, so that its volume forms a canopy of protection over the kneeling groups, and the upper part, curving like a bowl, is filled high with angel heads floating in divine glory. Here again is architectonic simplicity, allied with grandeur, in the distribution of the masses of white, rose, deep blue and golden yellow, and again an extraordinary interest of characterization.

The quality of intense, austere sincerity is represented also in *Miracle of S. Hugo* (p. 166) which is in the same Museum. Indeed, it is in Seville that you realise the nobility of Zurbarán's art. The examples in the Prado are by comparison commonplace; except the *Portrait of a Lady* in one of the upper galleries. This introduces us to the character of the artist's work after he settled in Madrid, whither he was sent for by the king. Portraits of women of fashion now occupied him. There is a good example in the Metropolitan Museum which, in pose and style of costume and low toned harmony, resembles the one in the Prado. In the latter, however, the silk fall of the drapery is drawn forward over the skirt by the lady's hand, so that its folds are more voluminous, and the whole figure, in consequence, is freer in design than the one in New York. As for the other picture in the Metropolitan Museum, *S. Michael the Archangel*, it is very hard to credit its attribution to Zurbarán. Where else among the artist's works can you find so palpable an attempt to imitate Raphael? It has nothing of the originality, breadth and determined naturalism that distinguish Zurbarán. If the latter really painted it, he must have done so in his student days with Roelas.

Zurbarán died in Madrid, probably in 1662. He is held in high estimation by the Spanish, but scarcely appreciated at his true worth by foreigners. To see him at his best, alongside of Murillo's work, as you can in Seville, is to be disposed to question the latter's claim to be considered the greatest artist of the Sevillian School. Certainly, as compared with Murillo, Zurbarán was more unequivocally the naturalist; he was at least as good a painter; a better, one may even think; and the qualities of his mind were superior. He had not the popular trait of sentiment and passion; but the higher gift of intellectuality and the rarer one of cold, dispassionate vision.

CHARLES IV AND THE ROYAL FAMILY   GOYA

THE PRADO

CHAPTER XII

GOYA

FROM the death of Velasquez, in 1661, more than a hundred years had elapsed when Goya made his début in Madrid. He is the unexpected phenomenon of the Spanish School; coming as a surprise and even more surprising in the character of his art, since it anticipated by a hundred years an art-motive of our own times. Goya was the prophet of modern impressionism, and arrived upon the stage when the drama of Spanish painting seemed to have been played out.

For the great names of the seventeenth century had been succeeded by painters of inferior ability and the positions of favor at court were held by foreigners. The decline of painting had kept pace with national decline. Spain under the Bourbon dynasty reaped the whirlwind that had been sown by the Hapsburg. Trade and commerce had been reduced to nothing; and while a few noble families had grown rich the country was poor, even the Court being impoverished. The Church had sunk from its high estate, and, devoted to worldly ambitions, had lost the respect of the community. The national character was demoralised. The lower classes had become brutalised, while society was callous and the Court openly profligate. When Goya entered on his prime, the impotence of the King, Charles IV, had permitted the government to slip into the hands of the Queen's favorite, the ex-guardsman, Manuel Godoy. He had been raised to the rank of Duke of Alcudia and made prime minister of the realm. For bringing to conclusion a war with France in which he had needlessly engaged, he ostentatiously assumed the title of the "Prince of Peace." It has been related in a previous chapter how he ratted to Napoleon and favored the design to place Joseph Bonaparte on the throne of Spain, thereby subjecting Spain to the horrors of a French invasion under Murat and to the prolonged distress of the Peninsular war.

Symptomatic of the moral atmosphere of the Court is an anecdote mentioned in Doblado's Letters. The King, surrounded by members of his household, was gazing from a window of the palace, when Mallo, who happened to be then first favorite with the Queen, drove by, handling a fine team of horses. "I wonder," said the King, "how the fellow can afford to keep better horses than I can?" "The scandal goes, Sir," replied Godoy, "that he is himself kept by an ugly old woman whose name I have forgotten."

. . . .

On to the stage of this shabby comedy of court life, set with the scenery of a nation's humiliation, Goya entered and made an immediate hit. A man of violent passions, without conscience or scruples, he played his part as if all the characteristics of his contemporaries were represented in himself. He has left a self-portrait, painted some seven years after his appearance on the scene. It now hangs in the Prado and might be mistaken for the portrait of a bull-fighter. Indeed, it reminds us that at one period of his young days Goya became efficient in the bull-ring. The neck is short and thick; the mouth fleshy and sensual; the nose broad; the cheeks large and heavily modeled; the cushioned brows indicate a hot, quick sensibility; there is a general suggestion of abounding animal force. Only the eyes, deep set and brilliant, proclaim the man's mentality. It is the face of a peasant, which in his origin Goya had been.

His father was a small farmer in the village of Fuentedetodos in Aragón, where Goya was born in 1746. Bred hardily and possessed of great physical strength, the boy asserted his independence early and, determining to be an artist, sought instruction from a painter in Zaragoza. Here he soon gained notoriety for his escapades and was distinguished among his fellow students for his daring and his skill in the use of rapier and dagger. Finally he was wounded in some broil and hidden away by his friends to escape the clutches of the Inquisition, whose attention had been called to the affair. Accordingly, after his recovery Goya found it convenient to leave Zaragoza. He made his way to Rome, where he stayed for several years, indulging his appetite for adventure and intrigue on a larger scale. He again fell foul of the Inquisition, through an attempt to remove a young lady from a convent and would have fared ill, but for the intervention of the Spanish ambassador, who promised to see that the offending artist returned to Spain. So in 1769 Goya arrived in Madrid. Shortly after his appearance in the capital Goya married the daughter of the painter, Francisco Bayeu. She must have been a lady of exceptional forbearance, since she remained true to him notwithstanding his frequent amours and presented him with twenty children.

Bayeu introduced his son-in-law to Raphael Mengs, who was in the height of favor at Court. This German painter, who had been invited to Spain by Charles III, owed his European reputation to his servile imitation of his namesake, Raphael. He was a facile, academic mannerist; drawing inspiration for his subjects from the Classics and rendering them with a purity of style that was absolutely bloodless. He was, however, sufficiently large-minded to discover value in the young Goya. The King had requested his Court painter to make an effort to revive the Royal Tapestry Works of Santa Barbara, and Mengs was engaging painters to execute designs. He gave a series to Goya, who prepared the cartoons which are now in the Prado. Some of them were executed in the weave and can be seen in a room of the Escoriál, adjoining another, decorated with tapestries after designs by Teniers. The latter's example may have influenced Goya in his choice of subjects, for he took the theme of popular pastimes and treated them naturalistically. The significance of this lies in its contrast to the conditions then existing. For the tapestries which were *à la mode* at that time both in France and Spain were the Boucher designs, in which little court gentlemen and ladies play at being shepherds and milkmaids, and indulge in pretty travesties of country life, under conditions of an impossible and ridiculous age of innocence. As we come to know Goya we are not

MAIA, NUDE GOYA

THE PRADO

surprised that this view of art had no interest for him. We find him to have been from boyhood an eager liver, interested to the full in life; so we do not now share the surprise that his contemporaries must have felt when they saw these cartoons. To a society accustomed to an art of academic imitation and rococo lackadaisicalness, they may well have been a shock. They seem also to have come as a welcome relief, for they made Goya popular; moreover they established for him a character of being independent, of which he subsequently took full advantage.

The color schemes of these designs are noteworthy. While the Teniers tapestries are based on a very naive use of the primary colors, red, blue and yellow, and the Boucher on a subtle use of the same, in which the sharpness of the hues is silvered down to demi-tints, the Goya introduce the secondary colors. They involve the red, yellow and blue, but merely as flashes of brilliance in a groundwork of plum-color, purple, dull brown-red, deep orange and blue, and rich greens, enlivened with white and velvety black. The schemes are intricate, varied, and above all, positive; the work of an artist with an original, if still unmatured, sense of color. Goya, indeed, proclaimed in this early work the fact that he was a colorist; although, as yet, there is little suggestion of the kind of colorist he was going to prove himself.

Following these cartoons came several commissions to provide decorative paintings for churches. Goya executed them in the spirit of popular genre that inspired the cartoons. Not only had he no religious feeling; he was bitterly and openly opposed to the Church, and in these pictures of saintly legends was at no pains to simulate a reverence that he did not feel. To this period also belongs the *Portrait of Charles III* of the Prado, which shows him in the costume of a huntsman, an angular figure with a genial but homely face. It is painted with uncompromising naturalness; the contours as hard and bold as the coloring; a picture separated from the Goya that we later know by a wide gap. The fact seems to be that in this portrait Goya was painting simply what he saw; and since the original was a man of commonplace exterior and Goya himself viewed him in a perfectly commonplace way he produced this astonishingly common-looking picture. It was necessary for Goya to discover some refinement in his own point of view, before he could develop his best artistic possibilities. The gradual steps by which he reached this goal I do not profess to know; but a few years later, when he had been established as Court painter to the new king, Charles IV, the true Goya is discovered. His new style, the result of a new way of viewing his subject, is fully developed in the group portrait of *Charles IV and the Royal Family*.

We will postpone consideration of Goya's mental attitude toward these royal puppets. That is part of his general outlook upon life, as a satirist and castigator of follies. It is his attitude toward his art which concerns us for the moment. The reproduction of this picture (p. 171) gives little but a limited idea of its artistic beauty, but it brings out the lack of human interest in, at least, the principal personages and the necessary stiffness of this arrangement of the figures. It will be noticed, however, that Goya has drawn the straggling items into some degree of unity by enveloping the lower part of the end groups in half-shadow. The eye is thus led to concentrate on the center of the composition. Here for an instant our attention may be occupied by the ungainly attitude of the Queen, and the forbidding expression of her face, turned, as in her other portraits by Goya, in one direction, while her eyes seek another. But it is only for an instant. Then we are attracted by the jewels in her dark hair and on her bosom, and by the exquisiteness of the costume—a fall of Chinese silk, mandarin blue, embroidered in white and gold, over a white lace skirt. Next our gaze may wander to the similar dresses worn by the princesses on her right, which however represent subtle variations of effect through the more or less of shadow in which they are veiled; and then to the king's rose-embroidered vest, the pale blue and white watered silk ribbon, and the stars and jewels which cluster on the plum-colored velvet coat. So gradually one becomes conscious of the loveliness of color that permeates the whole group, a bouquet of mingled quietude and brilliance, of low tones and sparkling keys, which one can enjoy with as complete a detachment from any thought of the figures, as if they were a parterre of flowers.

In fact, there is revealed here a colorist of extraordinary refinement and subtlety; and of an imagination that is rare among painters. Goya's original fondness for varied and positive colors has matured into a mastery over a few hues, treated with exquisite nuances. And the secret of this marvelous color-expression is the artist's new way of looking at his subject. He has become an impressionist in the modern sense. He stands forth, indeed, as the first of modern impressionists, the forerunner by nearly a hundred years of the principal art-motive of the nineteenth century.

. . . .

Goya used to say that his only teachers had been Velasquez, Rembrandt and Nature. It was from the first named that he learned to paint, not the subject in front of him but the impression he had formed of it; and in this he may have been assisted by Rembrandt's use of chiaroscuro to eliminate by shadow the unessentials and to heighten the saliencies by light. Yet it is difficult to understand how Goya could have had many opportunities of studying Rembrandt, since there is only a single example in the Prado, and the Dutch masters were not favored in Spain. Accordingly one is disposed to give Goya fuller credit for discovering his own way of rendering his impressions. As it is exhibited in this portrait group, it reveals an imagination that heightens the suggestion of beauty in the thing recorded, and an extraordinary gift of improvisation in handling passages of intricate detail and rendering the effect of an ensemble. There is no such maze of luxuriant loveliness as this in any picture by Velasquez; the nearest approach to it being, perhaps, the breast of the little Don Carlos on horseback. The Goya represents a more feminine sensitiveness; it is impregnated with temperament. This is the quality of Goya's impressionism which makes it modern. Velasquez's is impersonally objective; modern impressionism, like Goya's, is naturalism viewed through temperament; it shapes and colors the record to the artist's mood.

This is at once its weakness and its strength; a source of power when the mood is high and spontaneous, of weakness when the mood is slack or directly unsympathetic. Under the latter conditions Goya not infrequently turned out pictures in which spontaneity and imagination are absent, and the result is wooden, ineffective. Still oftener his faces are lacking in expression and in subtlety of modeling; while his hands, though one has heard them praised, are seldom expressive in modeling or in gesture. It was the *tout-ensemble* that interested him and in this the costumes play a very important part and are usually handled with incomparable mastery.

Two beautiful examples of his ability to encompass the spirit of a subject are the pair of canvases, representing a *Maia*, or girl of the people, in the one case nude, in the other clothed. In both the sofa is upholstered in green velvet, spread with silvery white draperies and cushions. But, in the case of the nude, the green is cool and bluish; in the other, a warmer apple-green to harmonise with the costume. The latter consists of a bolero jacket of mustard color with black and white lace trimmings, a white gown, shaded with tones of dove-grey and lavender, a sash of silvery hue, suffused with claret, and yellow Turkish slippers. The black network is laid on crisply and roughly, thus helping to set off the smoothness of the technique in the face, which has warm red cheeks and brown eyes. On the other hand, in the *Maia Nude*, the coloring throughout is cooler; a more delicate rose in the face, a faintly oxidised silver shadow under the chin and over the bosom; and similar shadows of inexpressible subtlety over other portions of the body. The flesh is cream with the faintest suggestion of rose; and yet not cream, for it seems to be veritable flesh. But, although this nude is painted with a naturalism that could scarcely be exceeded, the web of evanescent shadow in which it is clothed invests the nudity with a veil of idealism. These shadows, absolutely indescribable in their delicacy, are the result of a most perfect sense of values and of a technique as sure as it is facile. They are the despair of painters who try to copy the picture. Goya, in fact, in these two canvases, particularly in the nude, has caught the volatile essence of young femininity; has succeeded, as it were, in painting the fragrance of the flower.

Another kind of femininity, more matured, he has represented in the Andalusian beauty, *Doña Isabel Corbo de Porcel*, of the National Gallery. Here the technique, as befits the impression, is more brusque and vivacious. But in another example in the same Gallery, *Portrait of Dr. Péral*, Goya has adapted to the refinement of his subject a color-scheme and technique of unsurpassable delicacy. The features, pale pink, shaded with grey, are set in a frame of long whitish yellow hair; the coat is greyish drab, the vest pearly grey with green sprigs, the figure being placed against a dark olive-black background. The expression of the whole is of a man of rare cultivation and fine mental poise. The scheme of color recalls the *Portrait of Francisco Bayeu*, in the Prado, except that, in the latter, silvery blue is substituted for the green; this note of color appearing in the sash.

By the time that Goya reached his maturity the range of his palette was reduced to very restricted limits: blue, white, black, vermilion, some of the ochres and burnt sienna. And his tools were correspondingly meagre. Brushes of the rudest make served his purpose; or he would use a sponge or stick, securing some of his subtlest effects with the ball of his thumb. From several unfinished bust-portraits in the Prado it appears that he worked over an under-surface of orange-red; which no doubt accounts for the warmth and fulness of his greys. On the other hand, the subtlety which he succeeded in giving to all his local colors, laid on as they were in simple flat tones, is the result of a profoundly sensitive feeling for values. Goya's rendering of the varying qualities of light, as they affect the hue of a surface, is different from Velasquez's. With the latter, if one may state it briefly, it is rather the product of observation; with Goya, of feeling. Therefore, it is largely influenced by temperament, which makes it akin to the modern handling of values. In this, as in the character of his impression, Goya is a modern of the moderns.

It is interesting to compare Goya's equestrian portraits with those of Velasquez. Goya's best, in the Prado, are those of the King and Queen. Perhaps the most noticeable difference appears in the treatment of the horses. Velasquez, as we have seen, gave to each of his animals an individual character and action, suitable also to the character and psychology of the rider. A spirited small creature bears the little Don Carlos; a showy, powerful brute the swaggering Olivares; a beast, trained in stately menage, the proud and reserved king. With Goya, however, there is little apparent study of the structure or character of the animal; it is felt for its value as a handsome mass. And the rider's figure seems to have been felt in the same way; as if by emphasising its mass the artist could evade the inevitable commonplace of the face. Accordingly, in the case of the Queen, the impression we receive is of a black beaver hat with scarlet cockade, scarlet revers and silver braid on a black habit; black trousers against the deep green and gold of the pummel and saddle-cloth, and of a red-bay horse with darker tail; the whole forming a striking silhouette against a dull drab sky that deepens to slaty grey on the right, and a tawny, pale green landscape fading toward the horizon to silver buffs and olive. Similarly, the King's portrait suggests the effect of a handsome silhouette, which culminates in a blaze of splendor amid the decorations that cover the rider's breast. This is artfully balanced by the brilliantly white chest of the horse and by a paler white light in one part of the sky. Both these portraits, in fact, are primarily color-impressions. It is as if Goya had taken refuge in this point of view, in order to get over the difficulty of adjusting two such undignified personages to the monumental feeling of a large equestrian portrait. It was a case in which he tried to keep in control his feelings as a satirist.

QUEEN MARIA LUISA ON　　　　　　　　　　GOYA
HORSEBACK

THE PRADO

For Goya's role at Court was that of an audacious satirist, censor and chastiser of the follies and iniquities of his day. He was allowed a free hand, for his gallantry endeared him to the ladies and his prowess as a fighter made him feared by the men, while all, except the immediate victim, could enjoy the adroitness and daring of his humor. His particular *bête noir* was Godoy, whom he mercilessly satirised. He would amuse the idle moments of the Court by sprinkling the contents of a sandbox on the writing table, and drawing with his finger caricatures of the minister. On one occasion he appeared at some function during a period of Court mourning and was refused admission by the ushers, because he was wearing white stockings. He retired to an ante-room and with pen and ink relieved their whiteness with funereal caricatures of Godoy. Among the amours in which he indulged was one with the young Duchess of Alba, who returned his passion. Their liaison aroused the jealousy of the Queen, who banished the Duchess to her country home. When Goya learned of it he pursued his inamorata in hot haste and caught her up on the road, for an axle of her carriage had broken. There being no smithy near, he himself lit a fire and repaired the damage. The exertion was succeeded by a chill, which induced the first symptoms of the deafness that in later life became complete.

Meanwhile, the Court could not do without its Goya, and as he would not return without his Duchess, she too was recalled.

But Goya was far from being a mere buffoon and galliard. Although his passionate nature with its streak of coarseness made him at home in the petty intrigues of the court, he was a part of the wide-spread revolutionary spirit of his day. While Europe, and particularly France, was seething with the yeast of unrest, this solitary figure, far off in Spain, was already in revolt. In his denunciation of the hypocrisy and vice of his age, as exhibited alike in the Church, Society and the middle and lower classes, he was a Voltaire and Robespierre in one, brandishing the torch that subsequently kindled the French revolution. In this, as in his technique, he was ahead of his age. Meanwhile, the mental attitude which inspired him was characteristically Spanish: by turns grim and gay, humorous and deadly serious, coarse, sensual and cruel. In two series of etchings, *Caprichos* (Whims) and *Proverbios* (Proverbs), the scourge of his satire bit into the plates with a virulence of scorn and nakedness of exposure that have never been surpassed and, before his day, had never been attempted by an artist. In one of his etchings, a dead man has returned to life and is writing with his finger on the wall *nada—nothing*. Goya was a nihilist, bitter therefore against quacks and empirics, whether priests, doctors or lawyers. Also he laid bare the emptiness and horror of passion, a hashish that beguiles forgetfulness and leads to impotence and nothingness.

This idea of the nothingness of life in general, and of passion in particular is expressed with Goya's characteristic ferocity and lust of the horrible in *The Fates* (p. 182). Midway between earth and sky three female figures are floating, their lower limbs entwined so as to form a cradle, on which, with hands bound behind his

THE FATES — GOYA

THE PRADO

back and his legs screwed up to maintain a precarious balance, sits Man. Meanwhile, the crone on the left, a harridan of the slums, clenches in her fist a pigmy figure, whose hands are stretched in vain supplication to a darkened sky. Such is the beginning of Man's destiny; to discover the development of which another crone is peering through a spy-glass. The third Fate, nude, younger and of opulent form, turns her face to a lurid glare in the sky. Watching till the light fades, she holds the scissors which will cut the thread and precipitate Man, sated with passion, into the waters below.

This colossal travesty of life, as nothing but inchoate, chaotic, brute nature, swayed by elemental lust, is painted with such amazing brutality, that the pigments seem as if they might have been laid on with a trowel. The crudity is intentional, producing a texture that fits the monstrous irony of the conception. Moreover, before this picture one loses sense of color, as consisting of specific hues. It is, in fact, an apt illustration of Goya's own paradox, that color does not exist, that everything is light and shade of varying values. While one may discover the application of this principle in the meagre range of color, manipulated with nuances of value, which distinguishes all the canvases of Goya's maturity, it is particularly evident in his subjects of grotesque and violent imagination such as *The Fates*. Another example, selected for reproduction here (p. 189), is *The Scene of May 3, 1808*. The citizens captured by Murat's troops, in the riot of the previous night, are being shot down in batches; the incident taking place in the grounds of the palace of the "Prince of Peace"! The dull drab grey of early morning hangs over the scene and seems to have impregnated the uniforms of the soldiers and the clothes of their scared, hopeless victims. But the dead monotony is rent with a shriek, shrilling out in the clear, cold notes of the white shirt of the poor wretch whose arms are raised, in the yellow breeches and the crimson pool of blood. It is a remarkable example of color used solely for the purpose of expression; a use most characteristic of Goya, to which we will return later.

. . . .

In the troubles which overtook Spain, Goya proved himself neither patriot nor hero. He swore allegiance to Joseph Bonaparte and utilised the sufferings of his country for a series of etchings, *The Disasters of War*, in which the horrors of the military invasion are depicted with unexampled force and naturalism. After Wellington had expelled the French, Goya again played the part of opportunist and pledged his fealty to Ferdinand VII. The King, remarking that Goya's conduct deserved hanging but that he was a great artist and should be forgiven, restored him to his position of Court Painter. Goya, however, was beginning to decline. His deafness had grown upon him and with it a moroseness and irritability of temper, which made him shun society and bury himself in his country house. His deafness even denied him the solace of his favorite amusement, playing on the piano. His wife was dead, and the sole object of the old man's affection was his little grandson, Mariano, whose face he has commemorated in the portrait, now owned in Madrid by the Marqués de Alcañices.

Goya at length obtained the King's permission to visit France. He spent some time in Paris, where he was welcomed by Delacroix and the younger spirits of the French romantic movement. He then settled in Bordeaux, tended and cared for by an old friend, Madame Weiss. During this period he executed a few portraits and the lithographs, *Les Taureaux de Bordeaux*, in which his old time vigor is displayed. When the term of his leave of absence had expired, he revisited Madrid and was received by the King and people with marks of the highest respect and consideration. Goya was now in his eighty-second year, and returned to Bordeaux, where he lingered a few months and died in the Spring of 1828. Seventy-one years later his remains were removed from the cemetery of Bordeaux and interred with honors in Madrid. For by this time Goya's reputation had become world-wide, and his influence upon modern art thoroughly recognised.

. . . .

Goya's gift to the modern world is twofold: impressionism and, if one may coin a word, expressionism. To the former we have already alluded in comparing his kind of impressionism with that of Velasquez. While the earlier artist with his objective vision realised an impression of observation: Goya, influenced by temperament, recorded an impression of feeling. This attitude toward art naturally made him welcome to the French Romanticists, and through them brings him in touch with the general modern tendency toward self-expression. For the modern artist learned from Velasquez the principles of impressionistic painting, as a foundation of technique, but later derived from Goya the secret of impressionism for the purpose of expressing the emotion with which the subject inspired him. To the temperamental impressionist, therefore, Goya seems to represent the last word in technical distinction.

But to-day the impressionist himself is on trial. The world is beginning to question the worth-whileness of his art, except as a necessary transition-stage to something more fundamentally vital that is in process of evolution. What this will prove to be is at present in suspense; but we are vaguely discerning that it will be something at once more organically basic than impressionism and more spiritualised in motive. It may have been inevitable for the artist to depend on temperament in an age, such as the late century has been, of religious, mental and moral upheaval, during which the old academic, dogmatic forms of religion and art were toppling down, the hard old conventions that shackled social and mental betterment were being gradually disintegrated, and old values were being reduced to a flux in the melting pot of scientific analysis. But, as order has begun to emerge from this confusion, the need of a new constructive faith is taking hold of men's minds; the need of a new consciousness of some spiritual relation with the universe of matter. If the art of the future is to keep pace with progress outside itself, it must shape new motives to this need; and already there are signs that it is doing so.

It is here that Goya's second gift to posterity appears.

SCENE OF MAY 3, 1808   GOYA

THE PRADO

His influence has been working in the direction of expression, as the painter's goal, rather than representation. For a while, in the middle of the nineteenth century, Velasquez's inimitable faculty of recording a visual impression fascinated artists. Consciously or otherwise, these men were a part of the material and scientific tendency of the time, and material representation seemed to them the Ultima Thule of artistic achievement. Hence the thousands of canvases by men of all countries which in their point of view are neither more nor less than photographic. Their authors remained content to vie with the camera; and then, because they had superior opportunities in color, were proud and scornful when they beat the camera at its own game. Meanwhile, there were painters who began to wish to play a game of their own; to rid painting of the obsession in the matter of representation, and to make their pictures more expressive of their own abstract sense of beauty. To these men Goya came as a revelation. Through his impressionism of feeling they learned principles of expression, not discoverable in Velasquez.

It is true that the influence of Goya has tended for some time toward solely temperamental and emotional expression. That was because the tendency of the age ran in this direction. To-day, however, it is pointed in a new direction, facing the actual realities of existence. Impressionism is melting away before a new dawn of Realism. Thinking people are beginning to re-establish themselves upon the facts of life; not the old conventions that passed as facts, but the facts, as they are presenting themselves to a newly awakened realisation of an encompassing environment of spiritual facts. They are Realists, who would study the facts of life in their spiritual relation to the universe.

Behind this still uncertain momentum of modern thought art is groping. If one ventures to hazard a conjecture of the outcome, it may be that the painter will get back to a more disciplined and scientific use of form and color, using them organically, but not, however, to the sole or even the main end of representation. He will appeal as directly and exclusively as possible to man's purely esthetic perceptions, and correlate these to his conception of universal beauty. Painting thus may become once more, but in a new religious sense, a spiritualized expression.

Following this train of thought one comes upon a curious analogy between Goya and El Greco. It was no accident of changing whim that has made the progressive artist of to-day turn from Velasquez to Goya, and has drawn so many besides artists to admiration of El Greco. It is because both tender to the needs of to-day. Both are artists of expression. They share with Rembrandt the distinction of being the greatest artists of expression that any school can show. Though Goya's genius is confined to a lower level of expression, it points in principle to the spiritual altitude of El Greco's. Both are models of suggestion for the artist of to-day, if he is alive to the esthetic and spiritual needs of his age and is striving to express them.

That, after its own period of greatness, it should be thus refertilizing modern art, is the proud distinction of the Spanish School.

IN THE BALCONY GOYA

COLLECTION OF THE DUKE OF MARCHENA, PARIS

A POSTSCRIPT

VERY suggestive of the force and persistence of the Spanish character is the fact that the only Spanish artists of recent years who have become notably distinguished are those who have remained true to the traditions of their School. Academic encouragement has been given to the production of historical pictures, which cover large quantities of canvas but excite little interest. On the other hand, those painters who have acquired a European and American reputation have all based their art on naturalism.

The first of these in order of time was Mariano Fortuny, whose *La Vicaria*, better known in America as *The Spanish Marriage*, when it made its first appearance in Paris in 1870, created a sensation. The scene, it will be remembered, is a sacristy, profusely embellished with rococo decorations. The costumes of the figures are those of Goya's day; the actions and gestures piquantly natural and the characterization of each happily individualized. But the chief charm of the picture lies in the marvelous treatment of the light. Fortuny, after pursuing the academic routine and capturing the *Prix de Rome*, obtained an engagement to accompany the Spanish troops in a little war with Morocco. The splendor of Southern coloring opened his eyes to the magic of light. Henceforth his pictures became miracles of luminosity. The most powerful were *La Vicaria*, *Choosing the Model* and *The Rehearsal*; all rococo subjects in which the light is splintered into a myriad tiny reflections. But the finer work, in an artistic sense, is to be found in his water-colors. These are executed with extraordinary fluency and expression, marvels of naturalistic characterization, flooded broadly with glowing luminosity. Fortuny lived only five years after his remarkable début, dying in 1874 at the age of thirty-six.

Among those who were influenced by him, the most notable in imitating his virtuosity were Edoardo Zamacois, Antonio Casanova y Estorach and Fortuny's brother-in-law, Raimundo de Madrazo. On the other hand, the artist who has been most happy in uniting virtuosity with a gift of naturalism is Francisco Pradilla. He has painted decorations full of *joie de vivre* and the spirit of romance: popular merry-makings, camp-life and scenes along the sea-shore; spontaneous in execution, abounding with zest and aglow with color. Joaquin Sorolla y Bastida has followed in his footsteps, with a longer stride and heavier tread. His works have the zest of Pradilla's, but neither the refinement of virtuosity nor the versatility and subtlety of color. His naturalism is of the obvious type.

In contrast to him is Ignacio Zuloaga, an artist in whom has been reincarnated much of the diablerie and subtlety of Goya. Since the latter no other has dipped so deeply into the grotesqueries of Spanish life, while in a thoroughly modern vein he explores the psychology of his subjects. These include a diversity of types of femininity, subtly analysed and interpreted by means, particularly, of expressive color-schemes. Zuloaga, to-day, is not only the most characteristically Spanish of the artists of Spain, but the most advanced of them in his feeling for expression and in his faculty of rendering it.

Milton Keynes UK
Ingram Content Group UK Ltd.
UKHW030908151124
451262UK00006B/895